Praise for
The Feedback Imperative

"Anna Carroll has taken on a perennial organizational problem—the dearth of regular, constructive, empowering feedback that unleashes potential and enables organizations to achieve sustainable, quality results. Her approach to feedback is pragmatic, insightful, and energizing. As an experienced consultant, she knows the power of simple heuristics and tools to entice leaders into shifting their mindsets and trying out new practices until 'everyday feedback' becomes the norm. Carroll brings a 'lightness' to this frustrating topic, infusing her optimism and joy about the prospect of ordinary leaders becoming extraordinary by paying attention to and being accountable for this one focused area of their leadership. She powerfully describes feedback as an imperative and makes a compelling case for all of us to take seriously this essential human interaction. Our learning and capacity to adapt as individuals and organizations depends on it!"
—*Renee Rogers, PhD, VP, Leadership and Organization Development, Zimmer*

"*The Feedback Imperative* makes a compelling case that in the competitive information economy, leaders can no longer ignore their employees' need for frequent, honest feedback to help them focus & improve their performance. She clearly explains the pervasive reasons for feedback avoidance so that managers can recognize the assumptions, fears, and skill gaps that hold them back. She includes easy-to-use self-assessments and tools for making a feedback turnaround. Our leaders have benefited greatly from Anna Carroll's sound advice."
—*Bob Martin, VP, Covenant Management Systems*

"Many of us carry baggage about feedback based on early experiences with teachers, parents, and ineffective bosses. *The Feedback Imperative* offers tools that can help reframe feedback so that it's no longer something we associate with our fears about being judged, but rather a process that creates a space for rich, productive conversations with colleagues. The art of giving and receiving feedback is something every leader must practice."
—*Lisa Kimball, Executive Producer, Plexus Institute and Founder, Group Jazz*

"*The Feedback Imperative* is a must-read for every manager and supervisor, regardless of level. This book deals in a straightforward way with one of the most pervasive and harmful aspects of corporate culture and gives infinitely practical approaches to addressing the issue of lack of f...

s, *Executive Coach*

D1445634

"The insights, concepts and suggestions in this book provide solid direction for giving feedback. The valuable reminder, 'everyone wants feedback,' has sparked me to be more disciplined about communicating with my colleagues. Whether it is a simple email response or comments on a major project, sharing honest reactions can help build a team. *The Feedback Imperative* is an effective road map to achieve that goal."

—*Maureen Howard, Associate Vice President,*
New Mexico State University

"Everyday feedback provides a competitive advantage for executives and organizations who lead in fast-paced, complex, global marketplaces. If my clients implemented the frequent, transparent, and accurate feedback as Carroll suggests, their workplaces would see radical transformation."

—*Sheila Buechler, MBA, Executive Coach, LaunchBox Coaching*

"As the director of a small not-for-profit organization, this amazing little book provided me with valuable insight into many ways I could keep my team motivated and involved. Knowing how to incorporate simple feedback loops into the daily operation of programs and services makes everyone's job easier because they don't have to guess how they are performing and can freely discuss ideas to increase productivity. I implemented the COIN Feedback method as a regular item at our staff meetings to much success. Thank you!"

—*Celia Hughes, Executive Director, VSA Texas*

"The healthcare industry is changing and it's not just the delivery of care that needs reform. Healthcare leaders must remodel their leadership styles to meet the definitions of success in our evolving business. *The Feedback Imperative* demonstrates that we can no longer debate the expectations we have for our teams; expectations must be defined and feedback must be immediate. *The Feedback Imperative* helps us understand how to get where we need to be, quickly."

—*Carlton Inniss, Administrator of Hospitalist Services, Austin Regional Clinic*

"This is a book that should be a must-read at all levels of an organization; it is an important tool in front-line supervisory training programs. It is also an excellent reference for people at the executive level. While many books have stressed the need to give feedback, *The Feedback Imperative* addresses the roadblocks that prevent meaningful feedback and ways to overcome fears."

—*Elliot Kaplan, Director, Quality Assurance,*
Superior Completion Services

"Carroll's extensive consulting experience with assessing, coaching, and developing leaders informs the clear, focused approach presented in this book. She offers practical, detailed concepts that can be put into action easily to ensure that coaching by leaders includes the critical component of feedback. The tools and thought-provoking questions at the end of each chapter are particularly helpful for moving from key concepts to real-world application of Carroll's feedback principles. This book is an easy read with lots of examples that can help anyone who wants to improve their feedback skills at work, at home, or in social relationships."

—Dr. Stephen Schoonover, President, Schoonover Associates, author of the upcoming book, Adaptive Leadership Perspectives

"If you are a manager who wants to implement an effective feedback program for your team, this book's detailed, pragmatic approach will help you. The sample scripts, worksheets, guided exercises, and employee examples in this book will guide you to use your brain in new ways so that you can easily implement the best feedback strategy for your team."

—Katie Raver, Director of NLP Austin

"*The Feedback Imperative* spells out exactly what employees want and need in today's workplace! We see real productivity and engagement benefits from faster feedback loops as our leaders apply these techniques to develop team members."

—Aimie Aronica, Head of Technology Engagement, PayPal

"*The Feedback Imperative* is an important book for managers at all levels to read. The book's focus on separating feedback from performance review is spot on in its premise that daily feedback is not only critical to the success of any employee but also to a sound relationship between manager and employee; everyday feedback will nearly eliminate the stress that both parties typically feel around annual performance review time. By following the guidance in the book, managers become coaches instead of judges, and everyone wins, including the organization."

—Jeanette Cacciola, Senior Director, HR, Houghton Mifflin Harcourt

"Our biggest recruiting and retention challenge is with 'Info Babies' and I was immediately drawn to the chapter, 'Working with Younger, Ambitious, and Feedback-Hungry Workers.' We know that younger workers expect instant gratification and are very ambitious, but Carroll's explanation of how their expectations drive their need for continuous and rapid feedback helped me clarify not only how to adjust our recruiting tactics, but our fundamental assumptions about how to manage their performance so we can keep them engaged and employed. Any organization that wants to take advantage of the strengths of this new generation of workers would be smart to take Carroll's research and recommendations to heart. I know our future depends on it!"

—Mike McKeown, Director of Human Resources, Horseshoe Bay Resort

"The synergy of cloud technology and Agile software development is forcing technology companies to make shifts in development cycles, which are measured in weeks and months instead of years. Carroll's *The Feedback Imperative* provides essential insights, skills, and techniques for making that transition a success."

—*Marco Schneider, PhD, AT&T Labs*

THE
FEEDBACK
IMPERATIVE

HOW TO GIVE

EVERYDAY FEEDBACK

TO SPEED UP

YOUR TEAM'S SUCCESS

ANNA CARROLL, MSSW

RIVER GROVE
BOOKS

Published by River Grove Books
Austin, Texas
www.gbgpress.com

Distributed by River Grove Books

For ordering information or special discounts for bulk purchases, please contact River Grove Books at PO Box 91869, Austin, TX 78709, 512.891.6100.

Design and composition by Greenleaf Book Group
Cover design by Greenleaf Book Group
Cover Illustration: Ekapong, 2014. Used under license from Shutterstock.com.

Publisher's Cataloging-In-Publication Data
Carroll, Anna, 1949-
    The feedback imperative : how to give everyday feedback to speed up your team's success / Anna Carroll, MSSW.—First edition.
    pages : illustrations ; cm
    Issued also as an ebook.
    Includes bibliographical references and index.
    ISBN: 978-1-938416-65-1
    1. Communication in management. 2. Feedback (Psychology) 3. Employee motivation. 4. Job evaluation. I. Title.
HF5549.5.C6 C37 2014
658.45   2014939127

Part of the Tree Neutral® program, which offsets the number of trees consumed in the production and printing of this book by taking proactive steps, such as planting trees in direct proportion to the number of trees used: www.treeneutral.com

TreeNeutral®

Printed in the United States of America on acid-free paper

14 15 16 17 18 19   10 9 8 7 6 5 4 3 2 1

First Edition

For Mike, Ledia, Mason, and Walter

CONTENTS

Acknowledgments

Thank you to all of the clients, colleagues, friends, and family who have explored with me the possibilities of feedback loops, their promise for the workplace, and how leaders and team members can overcome the sometimes-hidden barriers to realizing their full power.

Diane Colvard has shared more than sixteen years of conversations about feedback and worked by my side in our consulting practice. I appreciate her extraordinary skill in helping me benefit from feedback loops personally and her great companionship.

Dr. Stephen Schoonover has been an inspiring mentor, teacher, collaborator, and coach to me since 1989. From the day we met, when leading sessions at the GE Technical Leadership course in Princeton, New Jersey, we have had fascinating conversations about feedback, leadership, competency-based development, the interplay of cultural values with feedback, and future workplace trends. Steve has helped me see a larger context for feedback, coaching, and leadership.

Renee Rogers, Vice President of Learning and Development at Zimmer and PhD in Adult Learning, has been my favorite and longest-standing client. An extraordinary thinker, researcher, walking partner, and enthusiast for new ideas, books, and ways of doing things, Renee got me hooked on brain science and has encouraged me every step along this book journey. I look forward to many more years of "talking walks" with Renee.

Also at Zimmer, I want to thank especially Nathan Folkert, President of Zimmer Trauma, for being the most feedback-focused leader

I have ever met. Nate has a uniquely effective way of selling the value of giving feedback and the skills for doing it to the leaders who report to him. I have learned immeasurably from our conversations about how he does what he does.

Mike McKeown has been a continuous evangelist for feedback in the impressive organizations he has served as HR leader, including Horseshoe Bay Resort where he facilitates leadership workshops that people find extremely practical. A naturally charismatic teacher and facilitator, Mike has collaborated with me in designing feedback-rich training experiences and applying team feedback approaches in the hospitality industry.

Thanks also to my professional coaching cohorts known as the "CTI Rockstars." All are great coaches who gave me amazing support when I told them about my book project. They are still coaxing me forward!

Great appreciation goes to my talented Greenleaf Book Group editors and experts: Brandy Savarese, Ashley Jones, Scott James, Matthew Patin, and Alan Grimes.

And finally, I extend very special gratefulness to my husband, Mike Wilkes, who believes in me; and, to my daughter Ledia, son Mason, and stepson Walter, who have provided non-stop encouragement, laughter, and pride in my work.

Preface

Shortly after I launched my career as an organization-development consultant in 1990, I became frustrated by a dilemma I encountered everywhere. I noticed the pattern so quickly that my notebook still smelled like brand-new leather, and I hadn't yet lost my stylish pen!

In my visits to companies, I would ask leaders about their business challenges and what bothered them most in their day-to-day operations. While their issues sometimes involved customers or groups outside the company, their toughest challenges were with individuals and groups inside the company. When I asked the leaders whether they had spoken directly with those colleagues in the company who could make a difference, the answer was invariably no.

It quickly became clear to me that frequent, honest communication—or feedback—among the people involved would be the magic ingredient a company needed to generate fabulous results. I shared this observation—my own feedback—and soon my clients agreed with the diagnosis and the solution. So far, so good, right?

But honest feedback was the one thing that people couldn't bring themselves to do. At least not when consultants were away. We convened meetings and retreats and used creative methods to encourage dialogue between the relevant parties. Those attending the meetings reached solutions and made action plans based on their honest, exciting, and sometimes startling conversations. Everyone declared victory from the business changes that arose from the feedback.

I witnessed how introducing feedback led to amazing solutions and built camaraderie. I saw how people began to work better with others after they exchanged honest information and created new and better solutions. When a boss was consistently honest and constructive with direct reports, for instance, everyone worked and felt better.

At the end of the meetings I facilitated, I almost always asked leaders to commit to exchanging feedback with the people involved with their goals. Although there is a natural reluctance for people to give and receive feedback, I thought the actual *doing* of feedback in our meetings had convinced them that it's so worth it. But when I checked in with them a few weeks or months later, I discovered that the magic ingredient had been ignored. Feedback had rarely happened.

It's not that people were scheming, hiding, or deliberately shirking their commitments. They had worked hard to implement the plans that arose from the feedback shared in the meetings. But two things happened: First, they got so involved in action steps that they *forgot* how valuable the feedback was as a vehicle to get them to their destination. Second, they simply preferred to do anything and everything *except* have honest conversations. They were very, very reluctant to actually give feedback.

While they willingly talked to their friends in other roles about the problems they saw, they avoided confronting peers who led other groups they needed to collaborate with. They maintained a polite distance to avoid pressuring people who were pulling in another direction. Instead, they reassigned roles and sometimes separated a few people out of the company. But they rarely talked directly with the people who could actually change the outcomes.

I saw the avoidance of feedback equally among leaders, between leaders and those who reported to them, between individual contributors, and between individuals and their managers. Feedback avoidance occurred to some degree in every single organization and relationship I observed—across industries, across functions, and across the world. It especially applied to consulting firms, law firms, universities, and nonprofits.

I saw the avoidance of feedback in my own behavior and within my work team. As I led teams of employees and contractors, I realized I was relying on them to shore up my own weaknesses and on myself to shore up theirs. Instead of suggesting positive changes that could boost their skills and performance, and asking them to do the same for me, I would sometimes shrug my shoulders and choose comfort over offering feedback.

Feedback avoidance is a human-to-human problem and it defies logic

The need for feedback is pretty logical. Whether you're trying to manage change, improve quality, boost performance, expand across the globe, find a better strategy, or achieve any important goal, you need more and better information from the people you work with in order to be successful. While electronic information about technology and finance is streaming in at warp speed, human feedback to help you communicate and learn to improve at your job is missing.

How can you change how you build and market products or serve customers if you don't know what bosses, employees, and customers notice, think, prefer, hate, and expect from you? How can you improve your way of leading if you don't know what the people you lead need from you? In addition, there are workplace dynamics today that make feedback even more necessary. Younger workers, it turns out, want way more feedback, coaching, and transparency from their leaders than any other generation before them could imagine possible. They are used to getting constant feedback from technology, and they demand it from their bosses.

The absence of feedback is illogical

I knew that feedback avoidance stemmed from negative emotions and not wanting to hurt or judge others. I knew it had to do with leaders' discomfort with these honest conversations. How do you open up sensitive topics and talk about them with people who may have already been reporting to you for quite a while? But until I researched the psychology of giving feedback, I had underestimated the brain science and belief systems that explain people's negative reactions to giving feedback. I hadn't fully accounted for the fight-or-flight responses and fears that hold people back from offering helpful feedback—based on their style, personality, and normal reluctance to inflict what they imagine as pain on other people. In this emotional swirl, who would want to give feedback?

Although I was seeing feedback avoidance everywhere I looked, I recognized the pattern from my very first steps into the world of organization development. I had started in 1984 as a social-work intern with social psychologists Robert Blake and Jane Mouton in their professor-like office a few blocks from the University of Texas at Austin. Developers of the Managerial Grid leadership model in the 1960s and explorers of conformity dynamics in the workplace, Blake and Mouton inspired me to see how company cultures worked—or didn't work—and how "culture" boils down to humans pretty much going along with the status quo rather than breaking out and risking rejection by the clan.

About the time I joined their company, Blake and Mouton had begun a fascinating project to explore why, in 60–80 percent of fatal airline crashes, someone in the cockpit had critical information—as documented in the recovered black-box voice recorder—that could have saved the flight. It was human error—the decisions made by the cockpit team of pilot, copilot, and first officer—that caused the plane crash. I was hooked by this discovery and got why learning and change had to occur as a conscious, deliberate choice, why it was messy, and why intense interaction between members of the tribe was required to make informed decisions in a confusing environment. I saw how poor decision making is proliferated and how we are all seekers of connection more than we are independent thinkers who make rational decisions.

Here was my first clue about how pervasive was the failure of honest feedback. I saw that the feeling of vulnerability and the fear of sharing a "different view" was so strong a force that highly trained people could allow planes and space shuttles to crash. I realized that a person's fear of disapproval from their boss caused professionals to allow flawed decisions to be made in business conference rooms across the globe. I knew that a huge force—human nature—was at work. Feedback avoidance was going to be a big problem.

I realized this before the surge of literature about emotional intelligence and neuroscientific explorations of the brain under workplace conditions. Now that the pathways of brain cells are being studied with the use of MRIs (magnetic resonance imaging), mirror neurons, visible through MRI scans that show the employee's neurons lighting up along the same pathways as the manager's, help us understand why an employee whose manager is feeling fear (or calm) is experiencing the same reactions. Fear of giving feedback begets fear in the receiver, whereas positive feelings about feedback encourage a receptive receiver. (Blake and Mouton would have loved the notion of mirror neurons at that time, as it explains why moods and attitudes are literally contagious!)

As a facilitator of group problem solving, I know what strange and interesting information can come to light. At one session, designed to increase collaboration between two major departments in a high-tech company, it was revealed that engineers weren't talking to production workers because of jealousy that had originated a decade earlier when executives appeared to prefer assemblers over engineers by praising their mascot—the rhinoceros—and adopting the factory workers' expressive, rhino-themed artwork and T-shirt designs for use across the company. After the story unraveled, the problems unraveled as well, and collaboration jumped forward.

In another company, the leader of one group admitted to not respecting the work of the people in another leader's group. He felt the other group's work was so shoddy that he didn't want to meet in the other groups at all. As a result, quality issues went unchallenged over many months. After going so long without talking about the problem, the first manager became too embarrassed to ever bring it up openly—until we had a feedback meeting in which everything came out. While there were hurt feelings and accusations, in the end both leaders focused on moving forward in the same direction, and quality increased dramatically.

In yet another company, it was revealed that some team members had remained silent while others had wasted millions of dollars on poor decisions. They realized that one or two influential people could sway the whole group into making a bad decision because the instinct to conform and avoid unpleasant conflict was so strong. After the feedback exchange, the team members set a new standard for welcoming skeptics' questions and avoiding groupthink stemming from feedback avoidance.

As a facilitator I provide a safe space for these conversations. Present for many honest revelations, I can't help thinking that if these "normal" but avoided issues can come out earlier, they wouldn't be perceived as problems later. Great feedback can occur in a safe space that is created by the individuals involved where coaching and decision-making conversations lead to amazing improvements in how the work gets done. Goals are achieved and a new level of engagement can occur between people who work together every day.

PART ONE

FAST, PLENTIFUL
FEEDBACK IS A MUST
RIGHT NOW

CHAPTER 1

Faster Feedback Everywhere . . . Except from Managers

As I heard my client, Gerald, explain that he was going to have to fire Tony, a recently recruited vice president from GE, it reminded me of similar conversations I'd had with other leaders about disappointing hires. Gerald's VP was veering off in different directions, focusing on the wrong priorities, and just didn't get the company culture. I asked Gerald if he had been giving feedback along the way, and whether the he had a clue about what was about to happen. Gerald replied, "Well not exactly. I just didn't have time to spell out everything for him. After all, he's in a very visible and highly compensated role, and he should know what we expect of him. He'll get a nice severance, and it'll be OK."

I felt weary. Stories like Gerald's, of people being fired from companies, were the most shocking. But there were hundreds more about employees still in jobs where they were underperforming, about people being tiptoed around and ignored by their managers, team members who were puzzled about why they weren't being developed or promoted, and those who were leaving or who had already left their companies because no one talked to them about how they were doing and so they were sure no one cared. There were stories from young and promising professionals who only found out at the end of their first year on the job that their manager didn't think they were performing so well. "What do you mean? Why didn't you talk to me about this earlier?" was their startled response.

The common denominator in each of these disheartening situations is little or no feedback. If I imagine a different era—say a hundred years ago—and envision how humans communicated with the people who worked for them, they may not have offered more feedback. But they couldn't have provided less of it than we are giving our employees today.

Digital feedback is omnipresent

In a world apart from conversations between managers and their direct reports, feedback is abundant. If you are a seller of game apps on Amazon or furniture on eBay, you can access a wealth of feedback, including statistics on your reliability and comments about your goofy game icons or the condition the rocking chair arrived in. Don't be surprised to see your exact words parroted back to you in an online review of how you handled a complaint on your toll-free number. Your customers' delight or frustration with their order is feedback that you can use immediately to improve your business.

Likewise, retail stores, credit card companies, call centers providing technical support, and businesses everywhere are collecting feedback and delivering it to the providers of that service—right down to the individual Apple genius who helped you with your slow computer or the hotel booking agent who accommodated your special request. By checking sites such as CollegeProwler.com, even college administrators can see how their school is perceived by current students and can address mounting complaints about their short library hours or shabby dorms. Doctors see their personalities dissected by patients on HealthGrades.com and other sites. Feedback about customer perceptions is available everywhere.

You're also getting instant feedback that tracks your progress on everyday tasks—such as filling out forms or buying airplane tickets. You can see that you are 50 percent finished with an online auto-insurance claim or note that three steps remain as you book an online ticket, by following a colorful graph at the top of the page. When you're lured into answering the multiple-choice survey on your online news site about which leader is to blame for the latest crisis, you get an instant summary and graphic display of how everyone else weighed in. Instant feedback measures such as these are examples of "gamification" tools borrowed from computer-game developers to let users know how they're doing at all times.[1]

So, what is feedback, really?

Although the term "feedback" is seen and heard everywhere today, whether in reference to online customer surveys or as workplace jargon for "criticism," it's actually a much simpler and more fundamental notion. *Feedback is information from past action that is used to guide future action.* The movement of the information from past to future action is called a *feedback loop.*[2]

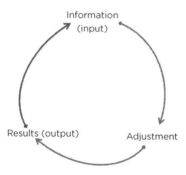

Figure 1.1. The feedback loop

To learn or change, feedback is essential. When you practice a new tennis serve, for example, your coach gives you information about how much lower you should hold your racket so that you can improve. In turn, you make the adjustment in your practice. When you change the way you serve the tennis ball based on the new information, you complete the feedback loop.

The more feedback we get, the more we want

One of the four principles of the gamification revolution in our lives is that rapid feedback cycles *maintain engagement*.[3] For example, using a Fitbit wristwatch or other gadget to track our fitness actions throughout the day motivates us to walk ten or twenty minutes more—to get closer to the ten thousand steps a day recommended by health experts. When we can instantly track our progress, we are fueled to try new behaviors, stick with our efforts longer, and have more fun doing them than if we don't have this information. We have accepted that a desire to learn is instinctual, but it turns out that we need feedback to fuel that learning.

Copious digital information satisfies this hunger in many aspects of our physical world. GPS satellite data gives us more confidence to explore places unknown. Weather predictions have become increasingly accurate in the last few years, due to more information coming in to paint a detailed picture of storm paths and wind currents. In 2012, Hurricane Sandy's path and destructive power were predicted with great accuracy by the data-rich projection model enabled by new technology.[4] Although destruction and power outages could not have been completely prevented in the locations where the storm hit, our new expectation is to be able to gather enough information to predict where humans will be safe or unsafe. We will never want to return to a time where we have less information.

In business, we rely on superfast information to design, build, and improve products and services around the world. The quality of Intel's chip manufacturing can be held to the same high standards in Oregon, India, Malaysia, and Vietnam because of the huge amount of information simultaneously transmitted between all of Intel's locations; in response, necessary adjustments can be made in the output from one plant to compensate for a need in another. With computers talking to other computers twenty-four hours a day, the supply of information drives better decisions about design, costs, schedules, sales, suppliers, quality, and every other aspect of a business enterprise. The more information we get, the more we want.

Similarly, in the workplace, everyone needs feedback information that will help them improve.

Accuracy is king

The usefulness of feedback is dependent on the *accuracy* of the information collected. If your tennis coach knew nothing about the sport and gave you random information about where to hold the racket, this bad information would be unlikely to help you improve.

In the hotel business, if your feedback comes only from guests who receive a free night in the presidential suite with its grand piano, marble floors, and a full view of the city, it does not represent your customer base and is therefore unlikely to guide you toward the most promising changes.

Likewise, if your manager deprives you of accurate information about your current actions and its results, you *both* will be deprived of better results in the future.

More feedback is better

If you're scouring eBay for that exact out-of-print copy of an illustrated version of *Three Little Pigs* that your grandmother read to you as a child, you may see that both Roger and Amy happen to have it in stock. Roger has a five-star rating, based on ten reviews. Amy has a 4.8-star rating, but it's based on twelve thousand reviews. Who are you going to buy the book from? Amy, of course, because you have way more feedback information about her performance; you are fairly sure that the book will reach you in good shape, while with Roger there's a feeling that you are taking a risk. New online customer-feedback systems capture data from a larger and larger percentage of the total number of customers so that the changes being requested are a safer bet for decision makers responding to the feedback. If you only receive feedback on one slice of data about your work, you will not know which adjustments will make the biggest difference.

The more frequent the feedback loops, the more improvement possible

If you are learning how to do West Coast swing, two-step, tango, or any other dance, there are multiple ways to seek feedback: by taking lessons from a dance teacher, by dancing with an experienced partner, or just by comparing your steps to a DVD. You would never try a new step only once. You want to practice it, get feedback on whether you are doing it well, and incorporate your feedback as you practice more. The more frequently you can cycle through your feedback loops of information, adjustment, and results, the faster you will master the dance.

The same holds true for learning on the job. The more frequent the feedback, the easier it is to learn and improve. The simple truth is that employees need more feedback from their managers. At work, a person's manager is their primary source of feedback information. If you are a manager, you may be the *only* source of feedback about whether an employee is doing a good job and, more importantly, what adjustments the employee can make to improve on a continuous basis.

Some employees get most of their feedback directly from their customers, from real-time reports about sales, complaints to a call center, or the number of bugs in their computer code. However, these sources alone—without input from their leaders—offer only a snapshot, not a full view of what is required of them in the role.

A manager's feedback role

If sales are down, there are usually multiple factors in play—targeting the right prospects, getting access to decision makers, diagnosing needs, presenting value that addresses customer needs, and so on. If you manage sales representatives, you can guide them toward better ways to utilize their time. For example, you may see that more preparation for meeting with high-dollar prospects will pay off. As you help the sales reps redirect their efforts, you can energize them along the way.

A manager must help each employee make sense of and prioritize all the information they are receiving, and continuously answer the burning question "How am I doing at my job, and how do I need to change what I am doing in order to improve?"

With more information flowing via computers and the Internet, there is now, in fact, more—not less—demand for every manager to provide accurate and frequent feedback to every employee. The feedback you provide has a multiplier effect on an employee's other sources of workplace information. For example, your team member, Marty, may spend too much time and effort researching a minor problem. But if Marty never receives your feedback, there is a strong possibility that he will continue to waste time that could be better spent on a higher priority. The larger the database of solutions available for Marty to search, the more your lack of feedback increases the amount of time Marty is likely to mismanage. Your lack of feedback creates a counterproductive multiplier: wrong priority, multiplied by a lot of time spent on it, equals huge waste.

Similarly, a globally distributed team working on a design project can spend days or weeks pursuing a direction that isn't fruitful. With frequent feedback from the team leader and feedback encouraged among the team members themselves, the team can clarify and correct their course of action quickly and reap the benefits of collaboration. With little or no feedback, they will have to backtrack and risk missing their competitive window. The negative multiplier here is misunderstanding multiplied by a large, diverse group working among different time zones, leading to wasted resources and even more misunderstanding.

Employees are starving for feedback

If you are currently a manager, it is probably the case that your responsibilities are diverse and you are pressured on many fronts. What you may not realize is that your team members are starving for the information they need to do better work.

Employees of all ages and ability levels want more feedback. In Gallup's massive longitudinal study on the employee engagement of workers at all levels and across the globe, there was no more important indicator of satisfaction and willingness to stay on the job than whether or not someone in their workplace (usually a manager) had talked with them recently about how they were doing on the job. A quarter of global employees in the same survey reported that they received no feedback at all from their supervisors, and this was a major factor in their workplace dissatisfaction.[5]

It would be easy to assume that the only kind of feedback employees want is happiness and attaboys, but this is untrue. In a study of more than 3,600 employees, 51 percent of them said that they received too little constructive criticism from their boss, and 65 percent of those who did receive feedback, either positive or negative, said they didn't receive enough information to know what to repeat or change.[6] People want to know *exactly* what they need to do to perform well on the job.

Gerald found a different answer

In the beginning of this chapter, I relayed my conversation with Gerald, who was on the verge of firing a recently hired VP. We chatted more about the impact of losing Tony, the VP, and Gerald became intrigued with the idea of trying *everyday feedback*—frequent, honest, and helpful feedback conversations—with Tony and everyone else in his management team. Everyday feedback places you in partnership with each of the people you manage and orients you toward your common goal of their improvement and development. Gerald gained insight into why he had avoided giving feedback and learned new skills for initiating and continuously offering feedback, and Brandon very much appreciated it. Gerald asked Tony for feedback about how he could improve his support and his overall leadership. Both began acting on the suggestions from one another. After a few months, Gerald realized that all of his relationships with the team members had become more positive, open, and trusting. Key decisions were being made faster and with beneficial results for the company.

Whether you are a first-line manager or an executive, the path to everyday feedback is the same and will pay off greatly for you and your team.

In the upcoming chapters, you will learn:

- greater insight about how your values, assumptions, and the emotional workings of your brain affect your ability to offer helpful feedback to others
- how to shift your emotional blocks to giving feedback into positive motivation and confidence in feedback as a success strategy
- six practical steps for implementing everyday feedback with your team members
- how to spread great feedback throughout your organization

EVERYDAY-FEEDBACK TOOL:
Feedback-loop diagnosis

Question 1: In thinking of your business, in what areas would you like to see the fastest improvement or change? *(Example: Need people to gain faster expertise with new technology.)*

_____

_____

_____

_____

_____

_____

_____

_____

_____

Question 2: For each of these, what information is missing for the people involved? *(Example: Less experienced people have little access to role models for feedback on how to improve.)*

_____

_____

_____

_____

_____

_____

_____

_____

Question 3: Of all the above, which area is the most urgent for your everyday feedback effort? *(Example: Faster launch of new products.)*

_____

_____

_____

_____

_____

_____

_____

_____

CHAPTER 2

Working with Younger, Ambitious, and Feedback-Hungry Workers

Younger employees are adamant about receiving honest, frequent feedback. Millennials, who will comprise half of the world's employees by 2014, overwhelmingly want more feedback than they are getting.[7] This is also true for some in the Generation X cohort—a smaller group born in 1965–1980, between baby boomers (born 1945–1965) and Millennials, or Generation Y (born 1980–2000).

There have been countless articles written about the characteristics distinguishing Millennials from Gen X and boomers, but for the purpose of understanding feedback preferences, we can merge younger Gen X members and Gen Y into a category I call "Info Babies," a descriptor based on the two generations' shared experience of growing up with real-time information at their fingertips. Widespread use of cell phones, Wi-Fi, email, and texting has made rapid-fire communication the rule instead of the exception for Info Babies. They are accustomed to sharing personal status updates, photos, or blog posts, resulting in feedback from their online communities within hours, minutes, or even seconds.[8]

For this soon-to-be-majority cohort of workers, information is free, easily accessible, and readily available. It's not surprising that Info Baby employees, accustomed to instant data access, also want instant access to crucial feedback from their managers.

I recently interviewed forty-six young technology and health-care professionals who were identified by their managers as "top talent" or "high potentials." Without exception, they preferred frequent, honest feedback from their managers. A large majority of them even desired more "negative" or "improvement" feedback, in the interest of learning more and succeeding faster, than they were currently receiving.

Typical comments from younger and "top talent" employees:

- "I want to know immediately if I need to change what I'm doing. I prefer managers who just walk in and tell what I need to do differently."
- "I can't believe that some managers wait for performance review to let people know they aren't good in a particular area. What's the holdup?"
- "Just lay it on me. I don't want to wait for feedback. And I want a manager who's open to my feedback, too."
- "I was hired in as a manager, a role I'd never had before. I'm lucky my boss pushes us to give more feedback to everyone—I get feedback on my feedback. My team is like a hungry beast. I feed them and they keep asking for more!"

Younger workers do not want feedback "lite." They want transparency.

In 2011, Jay Gilbert conducted interviews with Millennials that revealed just how serious they are about their feedback.[9] Responses such as this one were common:

> If I get feedback from above as to if what I am doing
> is ok, needs changes, should do more or less, etc., I do

not care about the message. I am very receptive even to quite negative feedback, but I like knowing where I stand, and I like knowing what the expectations are and how I'm stacking up.

Clearly, when it comes to feedback, younger workers want substance over style. The idea that a boss is softening or qualifying the delivery of a message seems foreign to them. It is not surprising that the employees most accustomed to unvarnished opinions, unverified "news" from a thousand sources, and emotionally "naked" personal revelations on the Internet want the same instantaneous access to unpolished, raw data—feedback—from their manager. And they want it now.

Continuous coaching

As Info Babies grew up, they became accustomed to parents who listened to and coached them regularly about their every pursuit. Even for those who moved away from home for college, boomer parents were available every day by phone. This phenomenon was the result both of the affirming parenting style of boomers, who grew up in an age of prosperity, and of the availability of mobile phones with no-limit fee plans, which reinforced the habit of having a mentor to chat with on a moment's notice. When joining the workforce, why not expect your boss to continue the always-available coaching?

The shift to radically transparent workplaces

"Transparency" is the word that comes up repeatedly when younger workers describe the workplace they desire and expect, and it comes directly from their experience of twenty-four-hour streaming information and their direct participation in the real-time information flow. This is a world in which texting isn't only an efficient way to coordinate lunch plans with your friend or after-school driving arrangements with your spouse. This is a world in which you are connected to hundreds of people throughout the day and night. Photos and personal information about friends, neighbors, teachers, and celebrities are not only easily available, but form the fabric of their personal landscapes. In the middle of a conversation between two people, one of them might text a third person to get the answer to a question the original two are curious about. If you ask me a question in a meeting, I will answer immediately, pulling up supporting data (if needed) from my phone or tablet computer. There is nothing to prepare and nothing to hide.

The huge cultural shift toward transparency in the workplace and consumer marketplace mirrors the life experiences of Info Babies. Many start-ups are coming out of the gate with a company policy of *radical transparency*.[10] Companies that are adopting this policy might also post everyone's salary on a wiki, share internal memos and videos with customers, post self-critique blogs when leaders make mistakes, and generally open all company information for employees and outsiders to see and comment on.

Clive Thompson, writing about the shift toward transparent workplaces, describes the real-life experiences of younger workers as a "cultural shift, a redrawing of the lines between what's private and what's public."[11] For Info Babies, authenticity comes from this kind of personal nakedness. They find it difficult to trust anyone who is cloaked behind so much preparation and concern for presentation.

Yet, the transition toward transparency is still in process. Although everyone in today's workforce is surrounded with technology, the three-quarters of today's managers who are early Gen Xers or boomers were not imprinted at an early age into the world of omnipresent information. While they may be OK with it, or even admiring of it, most managers do not share the same urgency for transparent feedback as do those who report to them. In fact, many managers today are more comfortable with a buffer of time to edit and prepare their messages, research on their own time, or withhold their impressions until they can appear better informed. Offering less frequent but well-documented feedback remains the norm.

So, performance reviews aren't enough?

Performance reviews are slow feedback, as they only occur once a year. Most employees do not want to wait fifty-one weeks to hear how they need to improve. More than 65 percent of all employees said that the feedback they received in their annual performance review contained "surprises" not mentioned by their manager before the review.[12] Unsurprisingly, employees become very upset when this happens, and it can be a factor in higher turnover. Although more and more companies now require semiannual or quarterly reviews, this feedback schedule is still too stingy and falls ridiculously short of transparency.

Where fast feedback happens

In companies considered to be the most popular places to work, feedback is far more forthcoming. Young employees are calling for feedback on a weekly or even daily basis, and the most innovative employers are delivering it.[13] For example, I interviewed a young manager at Twitter in San Francisco who, like his colleagues, schedules a feedback meeting with each direct report once a week. The feedback is two-way, with both the manager and employee suggesting behaviors they would like the other to "start, stop, or continue." Impatient with the annual review process, Twitter leads a culture of fast feedback, where no one is forced to guess what others are thinking.

Employers giving great feedback have a recruitment advantage

People want to work in places where their managers care about their development and coach them frequently, and where they will not be left to fail. In fact, a manager's willingness to give frequent feedback—both positive and corrective—is one of the greatest differentiators between companies where younger workers want to stay and those they want to get away from as fast as possible. Companies that merely provide an annual performance review will not work for Info Babies, who require real-time feedback and frequently scheduled face-to-face meetings about their performance. "For the average Millennial," write Joanne Sujansky and Jan Ferri-Reed in *Keeping the Millennials*, "feedback is indeed 'the breakfast of champions.'"[14]

So, why isn't feedback happening in most offices?

This all sounds good and, by now, you're convinced that workers want feedback and aren't getting it. So, you're probably wondering, "What's going wrong?"

There are many reasons given for why managers don't give honest, frequent feedback. Among them:

- Managers don't have time.
- Managers aren't trained in how to give feedback.
- Managers focus on their required once-a-year performance reviews.
- Companies are afraid that feedback will lead to lawsuits.
- Great employees are self-directed and can develop themselves.

While there may be some truth in each of these statements, the core of the problem is an emotional one: *Managers are simply reluctant to speak the truth to their employees.*

The pain of inflicting pain

Managers are human beings, and as human beings they are loath to inflict pain on others. They assume that giving honest, corrective feedback is going to cause hurt feelings, low self-esteem, poor team morale, or, at the very least, it will be a distraction from the manager's efficiency. Offering feedback frequently is even more painful, the logic goes. A few managers have candidly told me that they are simply incapable of giving people honest feedback and they would rather quit their jobs than do so. Other managers put it out of their minds and never even consider saying anything until they decide to fire the person. Still others have no problem giving corrective feedback, and they do it promptly and bluntly. But they may have avoided making the overall emotional connection needed to acknowledge an employee's strengths and help them develop from the feedback. The pain being avoided here is the personal relationship: "Hey, I don't want to get close to employees. I'm sure they can see my weaknesses, too."

Getting up the nerve to walk into an employee's office or call her on the phone may be excruciating. But the most interesting fact about feedback is that the one way to ensure that feedback is painful is to avoid giving it! What's more, the longer we wait to give feedback, the *more* it hurts both the employee and the manager.

The promise of feedback transparency

No matter what your generation, there is a huge upside to giving and receiving everyday feedback. In addition to keeping people happier on the job, feedback loops stimulate improvements and better results for the company. Referring to feedback and development of employees, Glenn Llopis lists the five most powerful things about transparency:[15]

1. Problems are solved faster.
2. Teams are built easier.

3. Relationships grow authentically.
4. People begin to promote trust in their leader.
5. Higher levels of performance emerge.

We are living in a critical moment in relationship to feedback. The information that a leader can provide by giving feedback has never been more sought after by today's employees, and yet most leaders and most companies have not fully awakened to this reality. Because you are interested in ramping up your understanding of both the emotional and business dynamics of feedback, you have a unique opportunity to steer the future for your team members, for your organization, and for your own personal development.

The remainder of the book is a guide for how you can realize the wonderful benefits of everyday feedback. After gaining even more insight into why most leaders aren't automatically giving feedback and how to get past those barriers, you will have an opportunity to try it for yourself and evaluate to what extent the leadership adjustments you make within your own feedback loop build the exciting future you envision for your group.

EVERYDAY-FEEDBACK TOOL:
Informal workplace-happiness survey

Instructions:

1. Conduct 4–6 interviews with a broad selection of employees in your group.
2. Ask about their engagement with the work.
3. Determine what's working well now and what managers can do to get better performance from their teams.
4. Ask yourself: What is missing in the area of feedback?
5. Summarize your findings in the following chart.

What's working well?	What's missing?
Example: Company has a sense of play and fun.	*Example: Feedback is infrequent.*
1.	
2.	
3.	
4.	
5.	
6.	

CHAPTER 3

Feedback Showstoppers: Skills, Support, Beliefs, and Brain Science

It's safe to assume that you are motivated to give more feedback to help your team members. You wouldn't be reading this book if you weren't. As a leader, you are navigating multiple worlds—your company culture, your team relationships, your personal management style, and your stress level. Any one of these can represent a serious barrier to you in giving feedback to your employees. For you, it is a feedback showstopper.

Which of the following showstoppers are the most challenging for you?

- **support** that may be lacking from your manager and in the overall company culture
- **beliefs** about how giving honest feedback will affect you and others
- **brain stress** from fight-or-flight hormones flooding your reasoning ability
- **skills** or best practices for giving feedback that you may not feel confident about

As you consider your showstoppers, you may feel overwhelmed at first. Most leaders can recognize more than one area of discomfort, and that's a great start. Recognizing the need for a whole new approach to feedback is an important step. If you consider your own situation more thoroughly, you'll also realize how much more is possible and how to build momentum for a positive "feedback turnaround."

As it turns out, feedback is a topic that is full of surprises. The parts that seem so difficult (like learning a good method for giving feedback) aren't so hard, while less obvious factors (such as stress hormones flooding your brain when you set out to give feedback) require brand-new approaches.

Showstopper #1: Support

The level of support you have for a fast feedback routine is dependent on the environment you inhabit on a daily basis. It's your company's culture and the way your bosses approach feedback. How are people typically managed—or mismanaged? How jazzed are the CEO and other executives about feedback?

Maybe your bosses are feedback avoiders. How often do executives sit down with the managers who report to them and coach them in an honest and helpful way? How often does your immediate manager, director, or VP talk to you about how things are going and how you each can improve?

The degree of support you have for giving feedback to your employees is shaped by your boss's way of doing things, the CEO's style, the recent and historical behavior of other leaders, and how much feedback is expected from people in their management roles. Are some managers who never provide feedback considered fabulous leaders and deserving of promotions? How conducive is your work setting for launching a more powerful feedback process?

If you feel there is little support for feedback in your organization, you are in good company. Based on research and personal experience in more than 250 organizations of varying sizes and global locations, I estimate that more than three-quarters of the companies' cultures are "feedback avoidant," as admitted by executives, midlevel managers, and most emphatically, by individual employees.

What if you don't feel supported in your wish to give better feedback?

What if the president of your company is horrible at giving feedback and avoids it at all cost? What if you are the CEO of a company with no history of feedback and the management team you inherited is feedback challenged? In these situations it might be easy to assume that feedback is unwelcome and that you should adopt the "feedback avoider" mind-set in order to survive in this environment. Maybe you've already given up on the idea of offering open, helpful feedback to anyone in the company. Maybe you are only giving feedback to your employees when it's required of you.

But does that attitude really serve you, your team members, or the organization?

First of all, most CEOs and managers are willing to pay lip service to the idea of better feedback. They may wish that their direct reports were more skilled at giving feedback to the employees they manage. The CEO and other executives may intend to give feedback, but somehow never get around to it. While they admire that kind of personal honesty, they aren't ready to make the change in their own communication style.

Doing feedback anyway

Just because leaders aren't ready themselves, it doesn't mean that they won't admire feedback done right, by *you*. I know, I know.

You're saying, "Why should I take this big risk when my bosses aren't doing it?"

The answer is simple: Feedback is incredibly powerful and it creates positive results.

The real truth is that no leader is ever fired for giving helpful feedback or investing in their people through coaching. And since everyday feedback leads to great results every day, your group will stand out for its excellence. Other leaders will be asking you for your secret.

Showstopper #2: Beliefs

Your beliefs and individual psychology also influence your relationship to feedback, as do your quirks, assumptions, and areas of comfort and discomfort. Are you an introvert or extrovert? Are you detail focused, impatient, sensitive to criticism, hyperaware of others' feelings, ready for change, or ready to run? Have you been a conflict avoider most of your life, or are you argumentative or short tempered? Are you only comfortable giving feedback to high performers? What are your beliefs about feedback? Is it scarier for you to give or receive feedback? Maybe you're not scared at all, but are you perhaps seen as threatening by others who misunderstand your positive intent to be honest?

Your answers to these questions reflect your personal beliefs about feedback, and your beliefs exert a heavy influence on how willing you are to give great, frequent feedback.

In order to dig deeper into your own personal beliefs and how these beliefs may have limited you in the past as you tried to give feedback to your direct reports, use the following list of descriptors to identify which belief systems are most relevant for you:

- **Analyzer**—organized and observant; values data over emotion

- **Empathizer**—encouraging and helpful; views corrective feedback as hurtful
- **Charger**—fast paced and results oriented; sees coaching as inefficient
- **Motivator**—visionary team cheerleader; chooses team versus individual conversations

These mind-sets are drawn from *nature*—the personality traits you were born with—as well as *nurture*—how you experienced parents, teachers, and leaders as you developed through life. Both nature and nurture affect how you approach feedback. Here are a couple of examples:

BJ: THE ANALYZER

Finance director BJ Crider is a true Analyzer who is uncomfortable giving spontaneous feedback to team members. He hates even the thought of giving face-to-face feedback throughout the year. Even formal, once-a-year performance review is very difficult for him! BJ's in a jam because several team members have recently made mistakes in their work with internal business customers and he isn't happy about having to take calls from his irritated colleagues. Although these errors have continued for a couple of weeks, BJ hasn't yet said anything to the team members because he's not sure how they will take it. Teri, who's worked for BJ for many years, has a tendency to get upset when they discuss problems. BJ just gave a raise to Marc, a "high-potential" employee who shouldn't be making these kinds of mistakes. BJ hasn't gotten around to saying anything about the problems. He is a feedback avoider because of his fears about how his employees might react.

MARTHA: THE MOTIVATOR

Martha is an enthusiastic leader who regularly motivates and praises the team in their frequent meetings. She has a clear vision of what her team can achieve over the next two years, and she enjoys getting people excited about it. Some job roles were realigned in an effort to advance their strategy. As a result, several employees found themselves in positions requiring new skills. Since Martha works closely with two of her direct reports, Chad and Chris, she sees their work every day and constantly provides them with coaching. She feels that she has built a strong bond of trust with Chad and Chris and can be totally honest about any issues. However, her other three team members are really struggling in their new roles. Martha hasn't spent much time with them and is apprehensive about providing any feedback that might be demoralizing to them or to the whole team.

Both of these feedback failures are hurting the company, the team members, and their bosses. Both scenarios resulted because of the leaders' limiting beliefs and the constraints of their individual feedback styles. To make changes, these managers will need to take a look at their own assumptions about giving feedback and consider how everyday feedback can serve them. They will need to stretch their ways of seeing the world and discover the ease of giving feedback and how to make it welcome and helpful for everyone involved.

Showstopper #3: Stress

The last few decades of brain research have revealed how much of our leadership and problem-solving ability is hijacked when we experience stress. If there is any element in the typical work setting that triggers stress, it is feedback. Having to give feedback to an employee challenges most leaders' feelings of safety, security, worthiness, and self-confidence. A leader unschooled in how to give everyday feedback feels the effects of their emotional, largely unconscious "lower" brain flooding the upper, "logical" brain with fight-or-flight hormones that send the message "Find a way to get out of this. It's very scary!" Not only does the overall feedback process suffer, but the stress drains brainpower for several hours after the feedback scare as well. It's a lot like experiencing a near-miss car accident that you dwell on for hours afterward.

The exact forms of stress experienced by leaders differ according to your belief systems. Some feel that giving feedback amounts to pain—either by inflicting pain on others who will feel hurt or angry when asked to improve; inflicting severe stress on yourself as feedback giver; or losing control of your time and flexibility in order to have time-consuming conversations with everyone you manage. This stress response associated with delivering feedback is now well documented by researchers viewing brain patterns of people giving and receiving feedback.[16] For instance, if you are an ambitious manager with very high standards, your discontent with personal failure may underlie your impatience with employees. The belief that "No one is going to make me fail" creates a strong fight-or-flight hormone response when an employee makes a mistake. You may want to fight—that is, tell the employee what is wrong and demand their compliance—while avoiding an honest two-way conversation about how they can improve. This becomes the opposite of helpful, constructive feedback and coaching. In chapter 5 you will be able to assess which stressors most affect you and learn ways to alleviate them.

Showstopper #4: Skills

Finally, there is the pragmatic "how-to" knowledge that many leaders haven't mastered. How do you start the feedback conversation? How do you incorporate examples? How diplomatic should you be when an employee is performing poorly? Believe it or not, this is the easiest challenge to overcome. Once you recognize the stress and negative beliefs that are getting in your way, you will truly want to change the way you do feedback. Then it becomes easy to pick up the skills. It's kind of like starting a healthy diet. Once you feel great about becoming fit and healthy, it's easy to learn the skills for choosing berries over brownies.

If you're like every supervisor or manager I've ever met, you've endured a course on how to give performance feedback. And every course starts with the admonition to do it regularly instead of waiting for annual performance reviews. But managers rarely apply the feedback skills shown in videos or described in books. You may see model managers demonstrating the "sandwich" approach to performance review (i.e., tell the employee something positive, bring up problem areas, and end with more praise), but this "principle" and other feedback skills go out the window when you are dreading the feedback experience. Nothing you see in training is useful if you're associating feedback with pain.

The big solution to the skills deficit is to overcome the pain problem. After you've had a chance to reflect on your beliefs, stress points, and sources of your pain, you can reset your association with feedback to a more comfortable and positive perspective.

In chapter 8 you will learn how to easily apply a four-step model as you move along the everyday-feedback journey. You can respect your own values (for great relationships, personal productivity, logical thinking, vision, and goal achievement) by actually giving—not avoiding—great, fast, and helpful feedback to everyone in your group.

Now that you are thinking about all of the factors that can influence your willingness and ability to give great feedback, you may be saying, "Aha! It's no wonder I find feedback to be one of the hardest parts of my role as a manager." You may feel the weight of all of these obstacles burying you and think you will never be able to crawl out.

But you should be encouraged now that you are about to learn how to roll these barriers out of your way. Once you're no longer looking in the wrong places to get better at feedback, you'll understand exactly which factors are relevant for you, and how to get on your feet and move forward with everyday feedback. You will be able to provide high-quality feedback to help your team members learn, develop, perform, and succeed.

EVERYDAY-FEEDBACK TOOL:
Your feedback showstoppers

Instructions: Rank from 1 to 10 how important these factors are as barriers to great feedback (1 being most relevant and 10 being least relevant).

_____ There is no time to prepare.

_____ It is hard to set up meetings with employees.

_____ Feedback is unfamiliar in our company culture.

_____ Feedback triggers fear and I avoid it.

_____ My direct manager does not emphasize feedback.

_____ I need more skills for providing feedback.

_____ I believe negative feedback hurts morale.

_____ People have worked here a long time and are not used to getting feedback.

_____ Honest feedback would discourage talent in this group.

_____ Other: _____.

Take a look at the areas you scored most relevant. These will be important priorities for you as you learn and adopt the everyday-feedback process.

Based on the items above, what do you need to include as you begin giving frequent, helpful feedback? Example: I need to explain why we are suddenly giving feedback after a company history of no feedback.

_____

_____

_____

_____

_____

_____

_____

_____

_____

_____

_____

_____

_____

_____

PART TWO

GETTING READY FOR EVERYDAY FEEDBACK

CHAPTER 4

Update Your Beliefs

Deep-seated beliefs about feedback affect us more than we might expect. Most managers agree that giving their employees helpful feedback is a good thing and resolve to do it more. But sometimes their personal values and assumptions undermine even their best intentions.

Your unique feedback beliefs

Are you more concerned with people liking you than you are with providing real-time information for improvement? Are you impatient with people who don't understand their jobs? Do you hate the idea of sitting down frequently with team members to discuss performance? Are you more comfortable working with data than emotion?

Your responses to these questions reflect your unique beliefs—some based on hardwired personality traits, others from your life experience. For instance, you may be an introvert if you get worn out by a day of nonstop conversations. Your tailored approach to everyday feedback must allow time for breaks—or it just won't happen. Some beliefs have been formed by your early experiences with parents, teachers, coaches, first bosses, and role models.

In general, your preferences about how you provide feedback to employees are based on the following:

- your personal assumptions about what feedback method works best
- what's comfortable and doable in your environment
- what actions will prevent negative consequences
- the Golden Rule, or how you would want to be treated if you were the employee

Although most leadership behaviors are based on similar assumptions or beliefs, the act of giving feedback may be even more influenced by the unconscious conclusions you have drawn from your life experiences involving confrontation or criticism. If, for instance, you're normally an assertive communicator, you may withdraw when it comes to feedback. A confident and charismatic CEO may not, for instance, want to risk being rebuffed by anyone who is openly critical of her actions—based on the CEO's having felt put down by a critical parent long ago. Another leader may feel that offering feedback to direct reports invites the possibility of being rejected—and this brings back unconscious memories of feeling unpopular in high school or college.

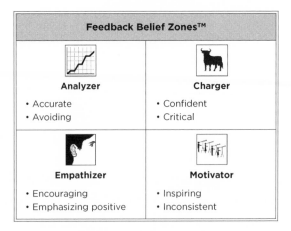

Table 4.1. Feedback belief zones

Four feedback belief zones

The four feedback belief zones are based on:

- Your degree of *introversion* or *extroversion*: These terms describe your preferences for direct interaction with others and your ability to draw energy from the people around you, or alternatively, your desire to reflect and draw energy from your own thoughts. (Note: There is no right or wrong here as both are well represented by leaders at all levels.)

- Your degree of comfort with *facts* or *feelings*: Drawing on facts allows you to reach logical conclusions, while drawing on feelings allows you to connect with people and communicate effectively. Both preferences are equally valuable sources of information for leaders to apply on the job.

The Extrovert-Introvert and Thinking-Feeling categories were originally developed in the work of Carl Jung, and have been expressed in many tools for personal development, including the Myers-Briggs Type Indicator (MBTI), Social Styles, Insights Discovery, and many others.[17] I developed the model shown here expressly for exploring beliefs about feedback, rather than for categorizing personality or overall leadership traits.

Four approaches to feedback

Empathizer

If your primary feedback preference is Empathizer, you are very much in tune with each of your direct reports' needs, feelings, and career aspirations. You have unique gifts for sitting down with employees and understanding their individual concerns and challenges. Employees trust you as a supportive and caring boss. You are comfortable sharing positive feedback with individuals, but your concern for preserving their feelings may delay you in providing the corrective feedback needed for improved results.

Analyzer

If your primary feedback preference is Analyzer, you have great skills in collecting accurate information about an employee's work actions, making observations that are objective and thorough, and drawing logical conclusions about the consequences of the employee's actions. But, because you are cautious about drawing incorrect conclusions and uncomfortable with emotional expression, you may not be forthcoming in providing frequent feedback.

Charger

If your primary feedback preference is Charger, you are more comfortable with giving prompt feedback about what is needed for improvement than those in other preference zones. You are confident and clear about business goals and you know exactly what is needed for success in your team. Employees can count on you to be candid, but you may also be perceived as critical, stingy with positive feedback, and unaware of employees' individual needs.

Motivator

If your primary feedback preference is Motivator, you are an inspiring boss and provide plenty of positive feedback to your whole team as well as to individuals who report to you. While you show a lot of support for your team members, you may be less patient in providing corrective feedback to help employees increase their impact. You are spontaneous and creative, but may lack consistency when it comes to addressing each employee's feedback needs on a regular basis.

Assess your own feedback approach

You may already recognize yourself in one of these four zones. Don't be surprised if you find yourself almost equally divided between two zones. Check it out by turning to the Feedback Belief Zones Self-Assessment tool at the end of this chapter.

Four primary feedback belief systems

The Empathizer belief system:
Positive feelings over objective facts

A leader whose feedback preference zone is in Empathizer territory is a born developer of people. They are skilled at encouraging people and recognizing their talents. However, at times the focus on positive qualities can distract from the need to provide constructive feedback that will help employees stretch beyond what they thought they were capable of achieving.

Feedback from an Empathizer feels good

Empathizers care, and everyone who works with them knows it. They are particularly skilled at connecting and communicating with individuals. As feedback givers, Empathizers are quick to recognize a person's positive accomplishments on the job, and they can accurately point out the details of how and why the employee's actions were effective. Those reporting to an Empathizer respond very well to their feedback and usually find it satisfying to work for a leader who acknowledges their talents and abilities.

Empathizers relate well to even the most difficult-to-reach people in their group. They are skilled at listening to each person attentively and getting why they feel the way they do—about their job, their daily ups and downs, their career aspirations, and even the family pressures and conflicts they are experiencing. Empathizers are approachable and willing to offer a sympathetic ear when a direct report encounters any kind of a problem—even when the employee is not accomplishing what is expected of them in their role.

If the Empathizer's approach to feedback could be characterized in a single tag line, it would be a quotation from *Mr. Rogers' Neighborhood*: "I like you just the way you are." Empathizers are affirming and help people see the value that they bring to the job.

Locating the Empathizer's pain

The Empathizer enjoys connecting for its own sake and finds it painful to risk inflicting pain on an employee by drawing attention to areas for improvement. An employee's pain is their pain, and they don't want to put their hand in that fire.

If you're primarily an Empathizer, you may visualize the scenario in which you give an employee corrective feedback: The employee has a painful reaction that results in lowered self-confidence and decreased self-worth. You just can't bring yourself to go there. While leaders in other zones may not imagine this scenario at all, it's a vivid possibility for the Empathizer.

Empathizers are also sensitive to the fact that they themselves have flaws that employees must put up with, and they are grateful to their employees for this tolerance. In the Empathizer's worldview, the leader and employee have a kind of unwritten contract in which they accept one another's strengths and weaknesses and make the best of them. The Empathizer may believe that pointing out the employee's weak spots will result in the employee pointing out theirs in return— another potential source of pain.

Possible risks from inside the Empathizer belief zone

Based on the Empathizer's approach to feedback, all or some of these risks may apply within their team:

- People aren't challenged to improve or develop beyond their current capabilities.
- Group results suffer due to the poor performance of some team members.
- High performers feel discouraged because poor performance is tolerated, leading to the attrition of high performers.
- Fast-track, highly motivated employees become bored or impatient with the lack of development and look elsewhere for a role with a boss who challenges them.

- Everyone in the group gets comfortable with lower standards and stops striving to improve.

Beliefs worth challenging if you are an Empathizer

Your primary feedback zone is accompanied by a set of beliefs or assumptions about what people need in order to grow and develop, how they will react to your behavior as a leader, and how you can lead them to deliver best results.

To avoid the risks of the Empathizer belief zone, it's necessary to become aware of what your beliefs are and be willing to soften or shift any that no longer serve you as a leader.

Belief	Soften It	Shift It
Employees rely on my approval to keep them encouraged and motivated on the job.	Employees like my encouragement, but learning and growing also motivate them.	My feedback encourages and also challenges them to improve their impact and increase their capabilities.
Feedback about what's not going well will feel hurtful to the employee and lower their self-esteem.	Feedback about how to improve is more helpful than avoiding or softening it. They'll be pleased with an opportunity to offer me helpful feedback, too.	Frequent and honest positive and corrective feedback is the most helpful thing a manager can do for an employee. Feedback between us is a great basis for a positive relationship.
If I save up the feedback until performance-review time and document it in the company's forms, employees will accept the feedback better than upsetting them with it throughout the year.	If employees get a chance to improve or change course based on my feedback, they feel better about themselves.	Employees benefit the most when I frequently offer positive and corrective feedback. Regular feedback allows them to improve all year long, which makes performance reviews much easier.

Table 4.2. Shifting Empathizer beliefs

The Analyzer belief system: Facts over relationships
If your feedback preferences align with the Analyzer, you see objectively exactly how employees can improve their performance. When it comes to feedback, Analyzers are methodical, careful, and concerned with presenting accurate information. The Analyzer's caution and avoidance of potentially emotional scenarios can hold them back from sharing the information they are so naturally gifted at gathering.

Feedback from an Analyzer is precise and thorough
The Analyzer approaches work from a thoughtful and detail-oriented perspective. Analyzers can work at the nuts-and-bolts level to make sure a project runs smoothly from the master plan to the fine print. As providers of feedback, the Analyzer is thoughtful and logical about when and where adjustments can be made to improve performance and chances of success. They are likely to have detailed, accurate information about the topic at hand. Team members benefit from Analyzer feedback because it is well thought out and objective.

Analyzers are observant and likely to understand the detailed inner workings of a project, which helps them relate to challenges faced by employees and collaborate on problem-solving solutions. Analyzers prefer to keep feedback on a professional level and avoid any form of communication that might lead to uncomfortable displays of emotion. The Analyzer views feedback as a transfer of information, rather than a personal exchange.

Locating the Analyzer's pain
The Analyzer prefers to stay in the realm of logic, reason, and rationality—a world where emotions have little place. Emotional

displays of sadness, embarrassment, anger, or frustration are extremely uncomfortable (especially in a professional setting) and an Analyzer would rather say nothing at all than risk the potential for an outburst.

If Analyzers are faced with a situation that requires feedback, they are likely to beat around the bush while trying to communicate an issue. Even though they might possess the perfect solution to a problem, the fear of being exposed and overwhelmed in the face of strong emotion is enough to make some Analyzers avoid the feedback process altogether.

Possible risks from inside the Analyzer belief zone

- Team members miss out on valuable information that could help improve their performance.
- There's a lack of face-to-face communication or regular team meetings.
- Deep-rooted issues may be swept under the rug or ignored.
- The Analyzer may take too long to contemplate an issue that requires swift, corrective action.
- Analyzers inadvertently create a cool, impersonal work environment that doesn't encourage sharing or connection with others.

Beliefs worth challenging if you are an Analyzer

If you're an Analyzer, you may believe other people's emotional responses are extreme or explosive. By using your natural powers of observation to note that this is not necessarily the case, you can focus more on providing your employees with frequent, helpful feedback that will achieve results.

Belief	Soften It	Shift It
Feelings are unbusinesslike and should not be part of a professional setting.	Although I don't prefer to focus on them, emotions are important for accurately understanding performance.	Rapport skills help me connect better with my team members and achieve even higher-level results.
I must understand every angle of a problem before providing any feedback.	I already have some essential information that will help employees improve.	Providing feedback and discussing solutions with employees will lead to increased success.
Vague feedback is better than honest feedback if it means that everyone stays calm.	When I provide examples and clarification, people know what's needed.	Honest feedback with full clarification is a positive way to work with all team members.

Table 4.3. Shifting Analyzer beliefs

The Charger belief system: Success over support

The Charger has an eagle eye on the target and knows exactly how to pursue it. Chargers have high standards and expect strong results. It's no surprise that their feedback style is bolder than most. When Chargers observe something that requires course correction, they are quick to point it out with the intention of driving results in the right direction. However, the Charger's feedback is often experienced as criticism and sometimes as an attack, because there is little effort by the Charger to gain the team member's understanding of a performance problem and its effects on business results. Employees working under a Charger leader will benefit from far more frequent feedback that includes time for give-and-take clarification so that the employee fully understands what will help them knock those goals out of the park.

Feedback from a Charger feels like being hit
with a cannonball

Rarely desiring a full conversation, the Charger may make quick, one-way remarks, expecting others to get the point and act immediately. The Charger is personally focused on high performance and thinks that team members are letting down the team if they don't automatically perform to the high standard—even if the impatient Charger hasn't clarified that standard. A Charger's team members may feel too vulnerable to ask their boss for help or guidance.

Locating the Charger's pain

Chargers don't like failure. They *really* don't like it. When a team comes up short or delivers substandard results, the Charger registers the event as a personal failure rather than acknowledging factors outside their control. Chargers see their own necks on the line in every project, and they attempt to mitigate any risk by requiring high standards of themselves and others.

Chargers don't like to see things go wrong, and they'll do whatever is necessary to make sure the job runs smoothly. If Chargers observe an employee behaving in a way that appears to threaten success (by proxy, their own personal image), they will not hesitate to zoom in on the error in order to resolve the situation.

Possible risks from inside the Charger belief zone

- Team members feel as if they are being held to impossible standards with insufficient support and mentorship.
- Feedback may be overly critical.
- Chargers may not see the need to combine feedback with coaching, personal development, and two-way communication.
- Chargers often lack the patience or skills to actively listen to ideas from another perspective.

- The idea of accomplishing a goal overshadows the development of people and processes that contribute to that goal.
- Feedback is quick and broad instead of more thoughtfully conveyed with details and examples that will help team members meet expectations.
- The Charger's fear of failure may become a reality if people avoid their Charger boss and feedback discussions never happen.

Beliefs worth challenging if you are a Charger

As a Charger, you have a certain set of beliefs about what it means to be a leader and get a job done right. Understanding where to adjust these beliefs will go a long way in helping you avoid the pitfalls of the Charger belief zone.

Belief	Soften It	Shift It
People should know their jobs and be motivated to perform them well.	People can use some guidance and encouragement from me all along the way.	Team members and I can collaborate through shared feedback to optimize everyone's performance.
I'm too busy to have long, in-depth feedback discussions.	If I spend time on feedback conversations, employees will gain valuable information they require to succeed.	Exchanging feedback with employees is one of the most efficient ways I can lead my team to success.
My team members should have thick skin and understand my quick corrections.	People can benefit from examples and dialogue about both positive and corrective feedback.	Regular feedback discussions that highlight success and offer tools for improvement build motivation for results.

Table 4.4. Shifting Charger beliefs

The Motivator belief system: Cheerleader over coach

The Motivator is the ultimate team builder. Motivators have a special ability to inspire others and develop strong commitment within their team. As extroverts, Motivators know how to communicate proactively. They are known for openly sharing their visions and goals. For Motivators, the feedback process is geared toward strengthening the team as a whole, rather than on individual development. Individual team members may feel that they are not receiving enough feedback or career advice from their Motivator boss.

Feedback from a Motivator feels encouraging but inconsistent

Often busy with other people, inside and outside the group, the Motivator is more likely to be found cheerleading the team as opposed to coaching each and every direct report through individual conversations. Working for a Motivator, you may feel like you're missing something when the Motivator forgets to deliver detailed information you need to succeed—especially when it's corrective feedback rather than a pat on the back.

Locating the Motivator's pain

The Motivator is threatened by the idea of discord and team splintering. At a deeper level, the loss of unity creates an uncomfortable feeling of failure and loss. Motivators feel as if it's their role to keep the team together, and they take it personally when the group dynamic begins to fracture. The Motivator's single-minded focus on group cohesion may take away attention from individual development.

Possible risks from inside the Motivator belief zone

- There's often a lack of consistent, individualized feedback.
- There may be too much spontaneity and not enough structure.

- Motivators might avoid critical feedback if it appears to endanger the unity of the larger group.

- Motivators often give shallow feedback, as opposed to the kind that's meaningful and in-depth, with examples and goal setting.

- Feedback loops may be left incomplete due to the lack of frequent, accurate information employees need to make adjustments in their behavior.

Beliefs worth challenging if you are a Motivator

If you're a Motivator, you may feel you're responsible for keeping up everyone's morale. When you challenge your own beliefs, you'll realize that team morale increases most when individuals are empowered to learn and improve.

Belief	Soften It	Shift It
I'm best at coaching team members I work closely with and don't get to the others as much.	Every team member can benefit from my everyday feedback.	Conducting frequent, everyday feedback conversations with each employee is key to my role as a leader.
The team could lose their morale if I bring up negative feedback.	Each individual will be motivated by helpful, positive, and corrective feedback.	We will have a winning team culture if we use everyday feedback to exceed our goals!
I must keep everyone motivated with my positive team spirit.	All team members can contribute to our positive team spirit.	Team spirit is highest when everyone is performing well and improving based on feedback.

Table 4.5. Shifting Motivator beliefs

No matter which zone you most identify with, take heart that as a leader you have definite strengths. Your strengths will be a huge asset as you ramp up your feedback efforts. Also, realize that every leader has some challenges when it comes to feedback and that you share with most other managers the desire to improve your skills. Awareness of your own challenges is a very positive step toward offering powerful feedback that enables people and gets results.

EVERYDAY-FEEDBACK TOOL:
Feedback belief zones self-assessment

Instructions:

1. Place a check mark before all descriptors that fit your approach to giving employee feedback.
2. Total the checks in each column.
3. Circle the name of the zone (from the four at the top) for which you had the highest total number of checks. This is your primary feedback belief zone. Read the section for insight into this zone. The column for which you had the second highest number of points is your secondary feedback belief zone. You may also wish to explore that material for additional insight about your approach to feedback.

Zones	Analyzer	Empathizer	Charger	Motivator
	☐ Observant	☐ Friendly	☐ Driven	☐ Cheerleader
	☐ Organized	☐ Encouraging	☐ Results oriented	☐ Inspiring
	☐ Has facts straight	☐ Good listener	☐ Assertive	☐ Mentors some
	☐ Collects data	☐ Helps employees and coworkers	☐ Can create conflict	☐ Fun
	☐ Slow to judge	☐ Tuned in to emotions	☐ Fast decision maker	☐ Postive future vision
	☐ Quiet	☐ Avoids hurting feelings	☐ Dislikes small talk	☐ Inconsistent
	☐ Slow to decide	☐ Smooths over conflict	☐ Impatient	☐ Gives some more, some less feedback
	☐ Sometimes finds people too emotional	☐ Overly tolerant	☐ Has high standards for self and others	☐ Downplays corrective feedback
	☐ May appear unemotional	☐ Avoids pressuring others	☐ Not tuned in to others' emotions	☐ Seen as emotional
	☐ Avoids conflict	☐ May be seen as emotional	☐ Gets to the point quickly	☐ May skip details
	☐ Sometimes gets tired of conversation	☐ Wants to be liked	☐ May hurt others feelings	
Total Points				

CHAPTER 5

Reduce Your Brain Stress

I've often brought up the topic of feedback at dinner parties with close friends, asking leaders at the table how they feel about giving feedback. They usually say they're bad at feedback and wish they didn't avoid it so much. Then the topic shifts. Everyone jumps in with story after story about crazy personal experiences when they *received* feedback from toxic bosses.

Feedback as attack

Feedback can be scary. Can you remember feeling attacked by a critical teacher, parent, or boss? Although the incident may have occurred ten, twenty, or forty years ago, you probably remember the painful blow to your whole sense of self. I still remember the words of my third-grade teacher, Mrs. Dangle, when she became irritated with my constant questions and comments in class: "Shut up, Anna. You talk too much and the others aren't interested." My self-confidence crashed, and it took an embarrassingly long time to recover from that assault. Many of us received a strong imprint about feedback from our earliest feedback givers—especially when those experiences left us feeling judged, criticized, rated, compared, humiliated, or singled out.

Fear in the brain

The traumatic criticism you received long ago has nothing in common with the helpful everyday feedback we're talking about in this book. But the "fear place" associated with criticism is where your brain lights up when you begin to think about getting or giving honest feedback. We associate feedback with criticism because our brains have labeled and stored feedback experiences in a "danger zone" category. Charles Jacobs explains this concept in his book about how the brain hijacks common leadership wisdom: "Our past experiences carry an emotional charge that is encoded in memories. When we encounter a situation similar enough to summon up those past experiences, along with their associated emotions, our prospective choices are marked by those emotions."[18] Brain research points to the hidden power of emotions as we consider options and make what seem like rational decisions.

Feedback triggers fight or flight

More recently, neuroscientists have been able to observe our brain activity during feedback. By conducting brain MRIs while people were receiving feedback about their performance on assigned tasks, the researchers were able to identify which areas of the brain were activated based on the release of brain chemicals. It turns out that feedback often triggers a fight-or-flight stress response. The threat of criticism triggers a flood of the same hormones that our brain produces when it experiences threats of physical harm to the body. The fight-or-flight hormones hijack our mental, physical, and emotional capabilities. Calm, rational thinking becomes impossible because our brain cells have received the signal to divert all resources to fueling our ability to run fast or fight hard.[19]

Who wins: Thinking brain or feeling brain?

The cerebral cortex, the logical part of our brain, is great for processing information that comes in through the senses, deciding where to store that information in long-term memory, and coordinating our efforts to solve a problem or complete a task. But, when faced with a stressor like feedback, it becomes immediately hijacked.

Who is the hijacker? In this case, it is the limbic system, the primal, pre-thinking, instinctual part of the brain. When aroused, the limbic system dominates all higher-order thinking. Always in survival mode, the amygdala—the emotional center of the brain—kicks into high gear, fires neurons, and releases hormones that help us locate and eliminate the perceived threat. When we get upset about feedback, the limbic system moves blood into our arms and legs and doses us with performance enhancers such as cortisol. It diverts oxygen from the memory and reasoning portions of the brain and disables competing efforts from the digestive and reproductive systems. This has the effect of impairing our problem-solving capabilities while the brain obsessively focuses on the perceived danger. An obsessed brain makes it difficult to attend to anything else. Decisions made while in fight-or-flight mode are rarely the ones we would choose under calmer, lower-stress circumstances.[20]

With all of this turmoil, it's not surprising that feedback is so difficult.

Giving feedback is at least as scary as receiving it

You might think that it would be scarier to be the one receiving the feedback than the boss dishing it out, but that's not so. Depending on your leadership style and personal assumptions, giving feedback may even be the more challenging experience. When you're about to conduct performance reviews with your direct reports, your brain makes an association with the emotions of receiving feedback and calls up the terror of inflicting pain on others. If you've ever implemented layoffs, you have likely observed an exaggerated version of this dynamic. Some bosses, faced with the task of firing people, become so physically ill from the stress that they simply cannot carry out the task without extensive support from Human Resources.

"Mirror neurons" make feelings contagious

It turns out that there is a scientific basis for the shared feelings among ourselves and team members. Emotional states are contagious!

The discovery of "mirror neurons" in the 1990s has changed the way we view human communications. Giacomo Rizzolatti found that when we observe actions performed by others, our mirror neurons mimic a subset of the neurons associated with performing that same action. Whether we throw a basketball or watch someone else do it, we are firing related neurons.

Mirror neurons also apply to emotional states. In starting a meeting, a leader may show nonverbal signals of anger—raised voice, exaggerated gestures, and a tense facial expression. That emotion is communicated to everyone else in the room, and the neural circuitry for anger is activated in each of the attendees. While this doesn't necessarily mean that everyone will become angry, it does mean that people in the group will share the feeling of tension or uneasiness.

Fear of feedback is contagious

If you approach the process of feedback convinced that you will hurt your team member, your team member is likely to take on your feelings of dread. Let's consider a performance-review scenario as an example of stressful feedback.

Your boss may have pressured you to conduct a forced ranking of all of your team members and insisted that you rate some with low scores. This pressure from above makes it uncomfortable for you to ask your employee, Jerry, to sign off on ratings he may find incorrect and insulting. If you feel stressed at the prospect of hurting Jerry, then Jerry will mirror your neuron activity and leave your feedback meeting feeling even more dejected than he would have felt with a calm manager giving the same low ratings.[21]

Emotions, emotions, emotions

If you approach any kind of feedback in a state of anxiety or stress, the others involved will be affected by your negative emotions. In fact, this pesky subject of emotions crops up in almost any discussion of feedback. It's no accident that today's leadership literature considers social and emotional intelligence as primary tools for success—both in feedback and in all workplace communication.[22] Your neurons are leading the neurons of others!

Further research on feedback shows that a manager's emotional messages are so strong that even negative (or corrective) feedback can be received positively when delivered in a calm and positive manner.

Calm delivery prevents the fight-or-flight trigger. Conversely, positive feedback delivered by a stressed-out or otherwise negative-sounding manager can be received negatively by the employee.[23] Either way, the manager's level of stress or calm is directly transmitted to the receiver.

So, what's a leader to do about all of this?

Everyday feedback offers some hopeful remedies that can move you beyond the stuck place where your brain chemicals take you. The great news is that neuroscience is showing us just how plastic our brains are and how they can adapt, change, and form new neural networks. Even deep-seated behaviors can be changed. The trigger that currently sends you spiraling into fight-or-flight mode can potentially be transformed into a manageable experience as the brain learns to relate to the idea in a new, nonthreatening way.[24]

Here's a plan

If you consciously focus on your own brain's ability to adapt, you can experience feedback in a far more beneficial way. Here are four steps to help you rewire your brain. You can experience neuroplasticity firsthand:

- **Recognize** any negative states of mind that feedback can trigger in your brain.
- **Reframe** the idea of everyday feedback as a helpful and positive action for you, your employees, and the organization.
- **Redirect** how you give feedback so that it creates positive emotional associations for everyone involved.
- **Revel** in your success as it will speed up the rewiring process.

Recognize your brain states

As you prepare to deliver feedback, notice when you feel stressed and uncomfortable. Take a few deep breaths, which will allow you to focus on your emotions. This practice of mindfulness allows you to observe calmly what's going on. Acknowledge that you're experiencing normal human responses to old associations that are popping up from your lower brain. Label your responses as "old stuff" and move forward with a more constructive view.

Bringing attention inward through the practice of mindfulness provides a window of opportunity to watch and learn instead of being swept away in the physical and emotional maelstrom of the threat response. This mindful attention leads to the creation of new neural pathways and more fully developed self-awareness, which in turn slows the knee-jerk fight-or-flight response when the unexpected comes knocking.[25]

Reframe the meaning of feedback

Now that you know the advantages of giving and receiving fast, frequent feedback, you are free to let go of the old interpretations you held about hurting people or wasting time. In the previous chapter, you identified your personal belief zone. With the knowledge that you're an Analyzer, Empathizer, Charger, or Motivator, you can form a new interpretation of feedback that serves your desire to support your team and accomplish your business goals.

Take a piece of paper and write down why you want to give excellent, helpful feedback and what it will do for your team members. Use the Brain-Rewiring Tool at the end of this chapter to differentiate your old associations with feedback from your new intentions.

Congratulations, you're already on the road to desensitizing your old responses to feedback. Brain plasticity is in effect!

Redirect your feedback actions

In the past you may have waited too long to mention a problem to an employee, resulting in strong frustration and anger by the time you finally walked into their workspace to address the issue. Now you know that you must initiate feedback conversations immediately and keep the goal of improvement in the front of your mind. In the next section, Six Steps to Everyday Feedback, you'll find all the details you need to redirect your feedback actions and create breakthrough results.

Revel in your success

OK, I know it sounds goofy to celebrate your success, but hear me out. There's a scientific basis in reveling. MIT studies have discovered that the brain's neuroplasticity can be activated subconsciously through the experience of success.[26] Imagine a feedback situation in which you and an employee manage to give and receive feedback that helps each of you become far better at what you do, in an environment that's fun and collaborative. That satisfying experience of success actually changes your neural associations with feedback. The brain takes note of what it did right and increases your motivation to give even more feedback.

You have begun a virtuous cycle: The more comfortable you are with giving feedback, the more effective you become as a feedback giver. As your feedback becomes more effective, you observe the positive results and become happier to develop employees through great feedback conversations. Less and less negative associations are present to trigger fight-or-flight brain chemicals, and voilà, the fear transforms into enthusiasm for sharing helpful feedback and asking for it in return.

EVERYDAY-FEEDBACK TOOL:
The brain-rewiring tool—a four-step process

Steps	Address each step
1. Recognize the state of mind that feedback can trigger in your brain.	Identify a few negative associations with feedback. Examples: Informal company feedback was harsh and created poor morale; most managers I've had avoid conflict. _____ _____ _____ _____ _____ _____ _____
2. Reframe the value of everyday feedback as helpful and positive for you, your employees, and the organization.	Based on your Belief Zone (Analyzer, Empathizer, Charger, Motivator) and your assumptions, how can you reframe your attitude about giving great feedback? Example: As an Empathizer, I can see that employees will be happy with improvement and career success that results from my honest feedback. _____ _____ _____ _____ _____

Steps	Address each step
3. Redirect how you do feedback so that it creates positive emotional associations for everyone involved.	What can you do to redirect your mind-set each time you give feedback? Example: Remind myself to stay focused on future vs. past behavior. _____ _____ _____ _____ _____ _____ _____ _____
4. Revel in your success as it will speed up the rewiring process.	Recall a feedback victory in which you and employees comfortably gave and received feedback. Example: I exchange feedback with two of my direct reports on a daily basis; we completed great projects. _____ _____ _____ _____ _____ _____ _____ _____

CHAPTER 6

Separate Feedback
from Performance Review

Performance review enters the feedback stage once a year with a lot of fanfare. It takes a bow, and in one big show it acknowledges a year's worth of work performance—good and bad. There's a lot of preparation time invested by bosses, with human resources directing from backstage and offering tools and props to ensure a successful event.

Performance review does have a definite role to play. But as feedback it is slow.

Lack of feedback is the number-one reason for performance problems. Many managers give feedback just once a year—at performance review. As retention consultant Leigh Branham points out, once-a-year feedback "is like a basketball coach telling his players at the beginning of the season: 'You're going to go out and play 30 games, and at the end of the season, I'll evaluate your performance.'"[27]

Employees get little or no benefit from the once-a-year performance-review process, as reported extensively in surveys and HR studies:

- A quarter of global employees report that they received no feedback at all from their supervisors, outside of performance evaluations.[28]
- Only 18 percent of American workers say they are given useful feedback from their manager during performance evaluations.[29]
- More than 65 percent of employees said that the feedback they received in their annual performance review contained "surprise" feedback not mentioned by their manager before the review.[30]
- Two-thirds of employees reported that feedback from their annual appraisal confused or demoralized them, and thus exerted a negative effect on their performance.[31]
- Millennials, who by 2014 will comprise half of the world's employees, overwhelmingly want more feedback than they are getting.[32]

Some of the rotten tomatoes thrown at the conventional performance-review process have to do with the unrealistic expectations people have for what a once-a-year feedback session is capable of. Most of us can recall a negative performance review experienced, not only because the feedback felt wrong and unhelpful, but also because we received a low—or no—pay raise based on performance ratings we didn't agree with. But, even if you have never had a horrible performance-review experience yourself, you—and 80 percent of all working people—are likely to have found the performance review inconsequential to your learning or to a meaningful pay raise.[33]

People trash the idea of feedback because they don't like performance review

As you build enthusiasm and get ready to launch your new and exciting approach to feedback with your group, the performance-review process can add confusion to your message. That's because performance review is often the only feedback employees are accustomed to receiving in a twelve-month time period. Performance review is the one moment in the year that every manager (OK, yes, there are a few managers out there who don't even do reviews) is required to provide feedback. Although annual performance reviews are probably required in your company for the purpose of allocating pay and keeping legal records about performance, they won't satiate your team members' hunger for real-time feedback, to talk to you often, learn and improve quickly, understand key goals, get transparency, or be recognized and appreciated.

Performance reviews are not collaborative conversations

The main purpose of a performance review is to document a legally defensible basis for pay and promotion decisions. Toward that goal, every manager is deputized into serving as a legal arm of the company. Certainly, meeting with a deputy is not the best way to build rapport and encourage employees to open up to learning and being coached.

For true learning to occur and for feedback cycles to get moving, the manager and employee must be on the same side of the table. But, in a performance review, the employee is definitely placed on the opposite side of the table from you, the supervisor. In such an environment, your direct report is not at all comfortable showing vulnerability and asking for help. Samuel Culbert, a performance-review contrarian, explains the adversarial roles set up in performance-evaluation meetings:

> You would think that the person in the best position to help somebody improve would be his or her boss. Yet thanks to the performance review, the boss is often the last person an employee would turn to. People don't want to pay a high price for acknowledging their need for improvement, which is exactly what they would do

if they arm the boss with the kind of personal information he or she would need to help them develop.[34]

What a disconnect! In all the current data about what drives engagement, we hear employees clamoring for a closer, more trusting relationship with their boss, and the standard performance-review process pushes employees and managers further away from trust.

Performance review is the ball and chain you drag behind you

To promote a beneficial feedback environment in your group, you need to recognize your employees' fears, which have developed over years of experience with unpleasant performance reviews. Although the association employees make between feedback and performance review was probably formed before they met you, it will color everything they imagine about any kind of feedback. As you tell them about your plans to implement a new everyday-feedback program, you will want to factor in their past associations with performance review and acknowledge them directly.

Performance reviews are exhausting for managers

These unpleasant associations between feedback and performance review may be even worse for managers than for employees. Pressures to rate and rank people, allocate scarce funding for salary increases, and complete laborious paperwork can wear down your energy and enthusiasm. Attracting and retaining great talent is hard enough without being asked to intentionally demoralize people.

You may find that performance review is an overly formal and rigid way to offer feedback. Daniel Pink, in *Drive: The Surprising Truth About What Motivates Us*, dubbed performance reviews as a "form of kabuki theatre—highly stylized rituals in which people recite predictable lines in a formulaic way."[35] You may be so worn down after an uncomfortable performance review that you never want to hear the word "feedback" again. What's so fascinating is that the very reasons performance reviews are draining can be prevented before next year's reviews—if you begin to have frequent, fun, and motivating feedback conversations.

I won't blame you if you can't quite see it yet. Adopting the everyday-feedback philosophy may not be on your radar screen as you struggle to complete your time-consuming performance reviews. Performance reviews may represent such a dark cloud for you that the bright sunshine remains hidden. Here's an example:

MARTY

Marty is a leader of ten people in a pharmaceutical company. Like many managers, he was disappointed with the mediocre results delivered by one of his direct reports. Marty felt that Terry, a product manager, had allowed her recent product launch to fail. It was time for Terry's performance review, and Marty needed to let Terry know what went wrong and why he was disappointed with the results. He dreaded that conversation and asked me, "How can I phrase this in a good way so that Marty will understand what I'm saying and not get upset? I spent hours documenting all of this stuff for each of my team members, but I don't think they can handle getting all of this feedback."

It became clear to me that Tony had avoided giving any feedback to Terry during the course of the product rollout. After helping Marty with how to stay future-focused in his review meeting with Terry, I asked him if we could set up a lunch meeting so that we could talk about everyday feedback—something fundamentally different than performance review. This feedback approach could help Marty and each of his team members. After Terry's review, we could start a whole new way of giving feedback that was easier, faster, and more fun. Marty, Terry, and all the others would have something positive to look forward to.

Feedback is way more important than performance review!

Performance review is overrated. It's gotten negative attention lately because of:

- procedures and evaluation forms that have grown longer and more complicated
- expensive performance-management software systems with insatiable appetites for minutiae
- company fears about being sued for wrongfully firing employees
- everyone's fear and loathing of an annual ritual that sends both manager and employee into a lower-brain fight-or-flight response

While there's an element of truth to the legal concerns about wrongful dismissal and some efficiency to be gained from an automated system that captures input from managers, the whole annual-review ritual is drastically overblown.

Everyday feedback is better

Everyday feedback, or "streaming" feedback, between manager and employee provides better information to employees so that they can adjust their performance every day in every way. It creates happiness for employees because they trust that their manager cares about them and coaches them frequently. It creates better results because the learning is implemented instantly. Surprisingly, everyone is less stressed.

Everyday feedback has very little to do with performance review. In fact, if you implement the six steps in the everyday-feedback plan, you can simply forget about performance review. You will never again need to worry about performance-review meetings. When you reach that moment on the feedback journey, you will be inspired to focus on just the right topics and lead the conversation quickly and without trauma.

Start this process after annual performance review

If your company's annual performance reviews occur in March, kick off the everyday-feedback process in April. You will be embarking on an exciting new journey, one that your employees have never experienced. Your goal is to put as much space between your new everyday approach and next year's performance review as you can.

If your performance reviews are spread throughout the year (i.e., held on each employee's anniversary with the company), make sure not to initiate everyday feedback within a few weeks before any team member's review. We don't want to create confusion or negative associations between feedback and performance review.

Everyday feedback is so much more powerful than performance review because you can tap into a motivation people already feel strongly about: learning and succeeding. You want to supply them with the information that makes improvement possible. Without everyday feedback, you are denying them access to the full information they need in order to improve. In a month or so they will be thanking you and even asking you for more feedback. You will feel relaxed and much lighter in spirit as a result of implementing your everyday-feedback plan.

How to break the associaton between feedback and performance review

Since employees see the concepts of feedback and performance review as intertwined, you will have to demonstrate why that association is erroneous through your daily behavior. With your own brain responses calmed down and mirror neurons signaling positively, you'll quickly send the message that giving and getting frequent feedback is a good thing. It will empower them to express feedback to you, and they will feel gratified that you are open to their views. The whole experience will be more fun, and it will allow them to shine at the time of their next performance review.

What about documentation?

So, what about documentation and HR records? Many managers have become so anxious about performance reviews that they feel that any kind of feedback, even the most casual comment made after a meeting, has the potential to cause an HR issue and trigger the need for them to complete a lot of required documentation. A few managers have become conditioned to avoid even the simplest offer of helpful information to their employees.

In reality, documentation at most companies is probably only required for a few occasions throughout the year or when a very poor performer must go through a progressive discipline process. Ninety-nine percent of the feedback that you will be giving in everyday-feedback conversations will not require documentation to be prepared for someone's HR file. In fact, there is less likelihood of anyone suing you or your company if you give them frequent, helpful feedback than if you deny them feedback, act standoffish and silent for 364 days, and suddenly spring a disciplinary process on them without warning.

Decrease the risk of managerial "malpractice"

The notion of managerial "malpractice" is much like medical malpractice or that of workers suing a company in a worker's-compensation disagreement. Studies have shown that "ordinary" physicians who communicate frequently, show respect for patients, and admit their own mistakes are sued far less than highly trained specialists who remain distant. Production supervisors who communicate frequently, show empathy with workers on the job, and welcome injured employees back (on a modified-duty basis) prevent worker's-compensation lawsuits that standoffish, silent managers unwittingly incur.

Likewise, any manager who coaches people frequently in an honest but supportive way is less likely to bring on a wrongful-termination lawsuit than managers who decide to fire someone without having ever offered constructive feedback. Even if an employee fails to improve, they have received tons of feedback messages all year about what is expected. If one of your team members sees that they're not a good match for the role, they are likely to take it upon themselves to look elsewhere.

In the rare circumstance that you must place an employee on a disciplinary program that may end in separation from the company, it is certain that you will need to collect documentation. But the every-day-feedback process, with its frequent feedback loops, will help you accomplish that more easily.

So, now that you are seeing the big differences between everyday feedback and performance review, you may be wondering how to act on it. In the next chapter you'll see that you have some explaining to do, and you'll receive some tips about how to convey the feedback message positively.

EVERYDAY-FEEDBACK TOOL:
Performance-review analysis

	Pros	Cons
1. What are the pros and cons of the performance review in your company?	Example: Forms short.	Example: Everyone ignores ratings; development plan is a waste.

	Strengths	Weaknesses
2. What are your strengths and weaknesses in giving feedback in performance reviews?	Example: I give specific observations.	Example: Sometimes I'm overly positive and they may not see a need to change.

3. How can everyday feedback make next year's performance review easier and more productive? *Example: I will be less stressed and more familiar with their work behaviors.*

4. How can I reduce the negativity that people associate with performance review through the use of everyday feedback? *Example: Employees and I will have a lot of opportunities to show improvement and learn new skills.*

PART THREE

SIX STEPS TO
EVERYDAY FEEDBACK

CHAPTER 7

Step 1: Explain What You Are Doing

If you're buying in to the idea of everyday feedback so far, you pretty much know *why* you are upping your feedback game. You believe it will benefit you, your people, and your organization.

But other people don't know that yet.

Sudden feedback after a drought is scary

If you start calling individuals into your office tomorrow and give them authentic feedback, they'll wonder what's up. They are accustomed to the old ways of doing things—a world in which their boss is silent about how they're progressing on the job. They're used to having to guess whether they should keep doing what they're doing. Your employees probably think that if you call them into your office to discuss performance (outside of their annual review meeting), they should be worried, very worried.

Are you firing me?

If you start giving feedback without warning, your folks may assume that they're about to be fired or put on a performance-improvement plan. They may not know that you're setting up feedback meetings with everyone, and they'll search for reasons why they are being singled out: "Why is she focusing on *me* all of a sudden?"

This is a predictable and normal concern. If you start giving feedback without warning, even if you're setting up meetings with each person in your group, individuals may not see that these meetings are being held for everyone in the group. This will cause them stress over the thought that their performance is not up to par. At best, they may think you're planning to lay off several employees at the same time! So, let's not go there.

Tell everyone at the same time

All of these unpleasant scenarios can be prevented if you tell your whole team what you are up to—at the same time. While you could send the details about your new campaign to give more feedback in an email memo, it's way less effective than telling them live—in a group meeting—with everyone hearing the same words at the same time. With a memo, it's likely that individuals will start wandering the halls asking one another, "What the [bleep] is going on here? I wonder if this is our boss's improvement plan and she's being told to do this by HR."

If everyone's together, you can answer the skeptics' questions more thoroughly—as soon as those questions pop into their minds. The shock can be contained in one meeting, leaving everyone to think, "Did you hear what I just heard?"

What to cover in your team meeting

Background

Tell them what led up to your decision to launch everyday feedback. Some team members were asking for more feedback and you realized that all of them deserve more coaching and support. You see that once a year is just not enough and decided that now's the time to start meeting with them to exchange fast and frequent feedback.

Let them know you will schedule initial meetings with each one of them during the first couple of weeks of this feedback campaign to give and receive feedback with them. Shortly thereafter, you will be giving more informal feedback on a weekly basis, and most of the conversation will be very quick and in the course of regular work. Remind them that you want feedback from them as well.

Purpose

The rationale for everyday feedback includes better performance, more development of their skills and knowledge, better morale, and more support. Everyday feedback will ensure that there aren't any surprises at their end-of-the-year reviews, as you will be talking with them frequently throughout the year about how they can improve their performance on key goals and other criteria used in the annual performance evaluations. Everyday feedback is also for the purpose of their providing suggestions to you about how you can be more effective as a leader.

Key points

- You are implementing everyday feedback as a positive step, not because you think the team is performing badly.

- You welcome their feedback and you are open to it every single time you have a meeting with them, as well as between meetings.
- Everyone will receive more coaching. Everyone will have an equal opportunity to learn and develop. Everyone will get both positive feedback and improvement feedback suggestions. Everyone's ideas for how you can improve will be welcome.

Employees' questions

What questions do they have? They may be shy at first, so you can prime the pump by suggesting questions they may have and answering them.

SAMPLE SCRIPT

Here is a sample script that several managers have adapted successfully:

Background

OK, now we're ready for the agenda item on everyday feedback and coaching throughout the year. I know this makes you kind of nervous because we have spent so little time on this feedback in the past. But I understand from our engagement survey—and a few of you who talked to me about it—that you would like to hear about performance issues and be coached earlier in the year than at the very end of the performance cycle.

I want to start meeting with everybody at least once a week to give you feedback about how you are doing and to receive feedback about how I can support you. Before you ask how the heck we are going to have time for it, let me just say my expectation is that after the first session, which may take thirty minutes each, feedback exchanges will probably take no more than 5–10 minutes per conversation. If you are comfortable with it, we will begin incorporating it as we see each other for other reasons. Some of you I don't see in person so I'll need to call you regularly. I will set it up more formally in those situations. With other people, I do want to commit to a feedback conversation at least once a week. If you prefer a set time, we'll try to do that. For others, we may naturally talk more than once a week.

Here is a suggested schedule for the first meeting—please get back to me to change or confirm these times. After that we'll set up a second meeting. After that we'll adapt the scheduling to make it efficient.

Purpose

My goal is to offer helpful, supportive feedback and coaching more frequently so you can learn and succeed quicker and so that our team improves faster.

Key Points

- The format for the first meetings will be to review any questions you have about your top goals and activities. I will include my observations of the work that you are doing—positive and "keep up the good work"—then we'll discuss some improvement opportunities and clarify what would work better.

- Once we get started and get comfortable with it, it won't be a big deal.

- Each of you will be asked to give me feedback. I need your suggestions, observations, and advice. I'm the one who is going to get the most advice because all of you are giving me feedback!

- None of this will go on a performance review or rating. You will have many weeks and months to change the way you're working and to learn new skills.

- I want to make sure this is an exciting and motivating process. Before the first meeting, let me know if any of you have any serious concerns. Make sure you come by and talk with me about it.

Set up the first individual feedback meetings for success

You may want to conduct the meeting in your office—only because you want to set the ground rules about no interruptions, cell phones off, and respecting time boundaries. Make sure that if you promised thirty minutes, you really truly end on time, if not earlier. Additionally:

- Move your chair to sit beside them with the desk or table in front of both of you.
- Ensure confidentiality of the meeting and of their feedback to you.
- Carefully record their feedback to you in a notebook or tablet computer. Do not, however, use any electronic devices for any other reason during the meetings.

Who to schedule first

If at all possible, make sure that your first few meetings are set up with people who are already good performers and eager, or at least comfortable, with feedback. You don't want to start this whole feedback process with the person who has presented the most challenges or with someone you've been avoiding.

Individual chats about feedback

Some team members may stop in to chat with you about the upcoming feedback sessions. You can get them relaxed by asking them what kinds of work items they think are most important in their role. You can reassure them that you will cover those items.

Then you can shift to a discussion about your request for feedback from them on the subject of how you could improve your impact. Kick off with a couple of items you think to be relevant (e.g., not yet fulfilling your promise to introduce them to some key experts they'll need to work with, or not answering their requests for new equipment or other resources). As you converse about the upcoming feedback meeting, explain the process in a way that highlights their point of view and the benefits they'll receive from it. If you have time and you've already thought about the topics you plan to discuss (see next chapter for examples), ask them if they'd like to have the meeting right then and there. You are demonstrating firsthand how easy and spontaneous everyday feedback can be.

EVERYDAY-FEEDBACK TOOL:
Feedback message planner

Instructions:

1. Write the names of people on your team and a summary of what each of these stakeholders think and feel about feedback now, and the message they need to hear.

Name	Summary of their views on feedback	Best message for them
Example: Casey	Casey wants kudos but also wants honest feedback.	Start with positives and sell idea of improvement.
1.		
2.		
3.		
4.		
5.		
6.		

2. Determine which points about feedback you want to make clear in you meeting with the team.

Examples:
- Assure them that they will have lots of opportunities to learn and develop.
- Each feedback conversation will cover no more than one or two areas.

a. _____

_____

b. _____

_____

c. _____

_____

d. _____

_____

3. Record your specific communication plans for how you will implement everyday feedback.

Examples:
- Introduce plans in meeting; cover purpose, logistics, and a preview of what they will experience.
- Follow up meeting by summarizing plans, and visit each person to discuss new plans.

a. _____

_____

b. _____

_____

c. _____

_____

d. _____

_____

e. _____

_____

CHAPTER 8

Step 2: Look for the "Highest Good"

To get moving with your whole new approach to feedback, begin by giving your brain a pleasurable task. Look forward nine to twelve months from now. Envision the most wonderful outcomes you can think of for your team as a whole and for each individual in it. Imagine everyone doing better work and using new skills. Although visioning may seem a bit off task or silly, I promise it will make you more, not less, focused. This will be a great way to launch yourself in your new role as your team's trailblazer through feedback loops.

In this chapter you will picture the road ahead more clearly. Your positive visions will help you select the best topic of conversation for your initial meeting with each person. You will soothe your brain with positive emotions as you see wonderful future scenarios unfolding. You will be ready to use the practice scripts you'll be creating in the next chapter.

Positive visioning is the opposite of stress

Envisioning positive outcomes has several advantages: First, it will make you happy. You will be making positive associations with feedback and rewiring your brain to see feedback as nonthreatening, even something to look forward to. If you bask in the images of what's possible for your employees, you'll feel the effects of brain chemicals that are far different than those associated with stress. If you're like other managers who are typically buried in problem solving and management details, you've probably been operating in at least a mild state of stress every day. The brain chemistry associated with positive visioning will have both relaxing and energizing effects, and will serve as a nice relief from your other tasks.

The second advantage of visioning is that it will focus you on how each individual can best contribute to your highest vision for the team and how you can optimize their talents and skills to make it happen. You'll know exactly where each person can focus their learning and which skill areas are not so essential to develop now.

The third advantage of your positive visioning is that in such a creative state you are more likely to access new ideas about how to bring together your team members' skills and talents in the service of your goal, how to get your people to help one another learn and improve, and how to better align everyone's job assignments toward big success for the team. There may be exciting surprises in store for many of the people on your team now that you're opening up your thinking to breakthrough success.

Visioning step 1: Prepare to relax

I realize this whole visioning effort may feel a little goofy. Just give it a try! There's a huge—I'll wager 90 percent—probability that you will like the results you'll experience. Here we go:

- Find a time when you have at least forty-five minutes to relax. Is it now? Later today? Tomorrow? Saturday?
- Use pen and paper rather than your computer for this task.

It will help you break any associations of your computer with spreadsheets and email.

- Download and print out a copy of the worksheet shown at the end of this chapter, which you can find in the tools link on www.everydayfeedback.com.
- Find a relaxing place to sit, preferably not at your office desk. It can be a comfortable chair in your home, at a coffee shop, or in the lobby of a hotel. It can even be in your car, parked in a scenic place.
- Disconnect from interruptions. Turn off your phone ringer and prepare to relax.
- Select a future time frame that would be meaningful to focus on—preferably nine to twelve months from today. Is it the end of the calendar or fiscal year? Is it at the completion of a project or deadline? Select any date that would be easiest to focus on in a positive way.

Visioning step 2: What's the "highest good" for your team?

As you sit back and relax in your chair, take three very slow and deep breaths. Use your creative brain to fast-forward to the future moment you selected for this vision exercise. If it will be in autumn, imagine tree leaves in beautiful fall colors. If it will be near the holidays, imagine decorations and holiday treats in your office building. If it will be July, imagine everyone coming to work in summer clothes. If there are off-site team members, include images of them during this season of the year, adjusting your visions for their geographical location— which may be very different than yours. Take some time to get the feeling of this future date.

Imagine the totally positive success of your team on this future date. See yourself with a smile on your face as you praise your team's success in a meeting. See yourself proud and enthusiastic about their capabilities as high-performing team members. What exciting goals have they accomplished?

When you can see, feel, and believe the positive results, make notes about what your team did so well. How exactly did they deliver great performance individually and together? Fill in as many details as you can in order to bring this vision into your sensory awareness. What are you hearing from customers and bosses? What can you see that's different: A much-improved product, dramatically better customer service, a streamlined process, a better P&L statement, or greater collaboration? How do you and various team members feel differently about your work? Are people more engaged and excited about their work? Are they independently solving problems and initiating improvements?

This exercise is meant to inspire you with possibilities and exciting achievements for you and your team members. Use the worksheet at the end of this chapter. Download the form from www.everydayfeedback.com to record images that depict success.

Here is an example of Sean's visioning exercise, ten months out, for his service team at the Red Pants Company.

SEAN'S FUTURE VISION: WAY BETTER SERVICE

My team of eleven successfully eliminated the major problem areas that customers were complaining about. Now our feedback from customers is great and I feel way less stressed! Red Pants customers reported that they got the service they needed on more than 95 percent of their calls. We are providing better online information, and we have become masterful in more areas of product expertise.

Everyone is learning and growing as a result of receiving feedback and coaching from their supervisors. There has been no turnover among the supervisors, and we've added eight new team members who are performing well. The supervisors coordinated to use both their own and their direct reports' knowledge to cross-train people. Each group created easy-to-use visual reference material on topics such as pants measurement, bulk orders for dance troupes, and fur tops. Everyone in our group is demonstrating their unique skills and talents and acquiring new ones every day. People help one another learn about future products and other new topics, and there's a feeling of win-win because our customers are served better. Product Design and other groups in the company tell us how pleased they are with my own team's frequent collaboration with them.

Employees are excited because they upgraded their skills and mastered more areas of expertise. Everyone is learning and growing as a result of the regular feedback and coaching I provide them and they provide me.

Visioning step 3: The highest good for each team member

Keep visioning. But now move on to imagining each employee's wonderful work. Sean did this positive visioning for each of his direct reports, and here are his notes for three of them:

SEAN'S STAR TEAM MEMBERS

Daniel

Daniel revved up his already polite and positive customer service to take on leadership roles. He learned how to field the most difficult questions coming into the service center. The group and I unanimously appointed him as our "Solutions Lead" in the center. When someone needs more training on handling questions, Daniel schedules a series of short meetings with them and patiently works with them until they are comfortable providing accurate answers. Everyone has expressed how much they appreciate Daniel's help.

Theresa

Theresa serves us well as a go-to person in her four areas of expertise. Two of these areas were new to her eight months ago! Theresa took it upon herself to ask colleagues, listen to others' calls, and read extensive documentation. Theresa learned methods for coaching her colleagues in a manner that feels helpful and not domineering (as she sometimes came across in the past). Now Theresa is considered to be especially collaborative and fun to be with, and other service staff members are delighted to work with her. Furthermore, Theresa receives extremely high ratings from customers, who experience her as particularly friendly and patient with their questions.

Marcus

Marcus, a technical whiz in the area of online ordering issues, dramatically improved his rapport-building skills by moderating his tone, using key phrases to soothe irritated customers, and explaining the technical information in a simpler, step-by-step manner. We also leveraged his knowledge of advanced concepts so that other people could access answers more easily. Marcus's enjoyment of structure and creating online tools is a great resource to the group, and we are thrilled that he wants to continue applying those skills in the coming year to help everyone learn more and more.

If you are working with a team of managers, you can envision success that cascades down through multiple levels. Sandy, a vice president, had this positive vision for his marketing group:

WONDERFUL MANAGEMENT TEAM

My management team raised the bar for how to engage and develop employees. We set coordinated goals for the whole team and ensured that each manager in the team understood and could articulate our goals to people in their group. Then they went out and did just that. Some of their direct reports were coming up to me and telling me that this was the first time they ever understood what everyone in our larger group did. One of our goals was celebrating and motivating people through fun group events. We kicked off the year with a series of small team lunches, planned and customized by each manager and people they appointed as "planners."

On the accomplishment front, we set up targets and measures and visually displayed them as large, graphic charts in our front hall and online—to ensure that we were consistent and accountable. Each manager implemented everyday feedback consistently across our whole group. Every single employee in this group has experienced a ramp-up in leadership. In fact, we just completed a short survey. The before and after scores show dramatic gains in team members' engagement and excitement about working for this company!

WONDERFUL MANAGEMENT TEAM MEMBERS

Jill

Jill understands and appreciates the value of having regular team meetings for communicating with her whole group. She began delegating responsibilities among her team members to tap into each individual's full capabilities and interests. This is a great step for her, as she had been considered by some in her group as a micromanager. She is now even rotating the leadership of her weekly meeting so that everyone in the team has a turn at facilitating. We have drawn on her great skills in project management to ensure that her peers and their teams are consistent about documenting what their team members are doing.

Andrew

Andrew's infectiously positive communication style has helped all of our managers (and me) get ideas on how to attract and retain motivated team members. He shared with us how he communicates with his work group in such an effective manner, using humor, great listening skills, and constant recognition of people's great work. He has started using his talents to help his group sell solutions to the other departments they work with, rather than waiting for problem calls. Andrew has also provided more regular communications with his remote team members so that everyone stays coordinated rather than isolated, as they have felt in the past.

Positive feedback is not just nicey-nice

You may still subconsciously feel that the word "feedback" means negative feedback or it would just be called "praise." Recall the whole idea of feedback loops as information that is used to adjust a process. "Positive" feedback is just as essential as "corrective" feedback to adjust the process. Think of a time when you or others in your group solved a problem in a unique way or inadvertently took a different approach and it turned out to be a breakthrough innovation. If you didn't recognize the results of that effort and consciously plan to repeat it, you'd have lost out on the crucial informational benefit of feedback.

A simple example occurred a few decades ago at one property in a large hotel chain. Someone brought a huge batch of cookies to work and handed them out to customers and employees. The hotel received so many positive comments from the customers that they implemented the cookie treats as part of their brand strategy across the whole chain. You've probably had one yourself!

Believe it or not, most people take for granted what comes naturally or easily for them. Even if they're in the top one percent of the population in, say, databases, teaching customers, or dealing with conflict, they may not necessarily see how it impacts the company so positively. They aren't aware of how special their capabilities are, and they may even be impatient with others who don't naturally have the same skills. Everyday feedback offers you the opportunity to ask them to do more of what's good, to let go of their other priorities, and even to ask them to coach others in learning and applying the same "easy" skills.

Notice the number of positive results in these visioning examples. Notice how individuals' natural skills were leveraged to benefit the team. Of course, for every employee, there are usually a few areas that are hard to develop, and after six to twelve months, you will still see room for improvement. In your vision for each person, incorporate how they will develop and apply new skills and make improvements to their business process as soon as possible. Envision them turning around problems or suboptimal behaviors in exchange for actions that work far better.

Get focused on feedback topics

Finally, we are looping around to answer the big question: What does all this visioning have to do with feedback? By now, I hope you notice that one or two of the right changes from each person would make a gigantic difference to your team's success. So now, let's translate your vision into usable bites of feedback.

Be smart about which bites of improvement feedback will make the most difference for each team member's success. What are some things you think they can change fairly easily to make a huge difference? Consider what would be the easiest skill for them to learn or improve upon and what requires more time, education, or practice. If you're stumped on how to prioritize potential feedback topics for someone on your team, use Table 8.1. Draw a large square on paper and divide it into four parts. After brainstorming some areas the person needs to improve, record those areas in the appropriate box.

Choosing feedback topics

	High / Difficult or long Worth developing over time Don't bite off too many of these	High / Easy or moderate Great topics for initial feedback
	Low / Hard to modify Very bad idea Poor use of time	Low / Easy to modify Distraction Need to refocus person on higher-impact results

Impact on Results — High / Low

Ease of Change
Harder ◄──────► Easier

Table 8.1. Choosing feedback topics. Pick a few skills or capabilities from the upper right corner, and identify no more than one area in the top left box.

Proper bite size

Feedback is ideal if it is focused on understandable and doable bites. Daniel Pink draws on research into optimal flow states to identify the conditions in which people achieve great things in the easiest manner. A key condition he describes is making "Goldilocks-sized" goals: not too hard, not too easy, just right.[36] When choosing your feedback bites, make sure not to overwhelm your employee with a huge, unreachable learning goal. But make sure it's something big enough to make a real difference in their work and make them feel proud.

Use the end-of-chapter worksheet to record some feedback bites for each person that are most promising for getting results. We will use this information in chapter 9 to create feedback prompts for your everyday-feedback conversations.

Finally, notice how much you accomplished in this exercise. Although it may have felt hokey at first, reflect on how positive visioning guided you to see the highest priorities for feedback to each person. Notice how some behaviors you've observed employees doing just didn't come up as high priority and other capabilities can be phased in over time. That's OK and normal. In fact, it's a good thing: Your actual feedback conversations will be easier than you thought. You won't need to nitpick in areas that don't really drive results for the team, and you can save some of the longer-term improvements—e.g., "get an engineering degree"—until later. You are now being more strategic about how you will give feedback and coach people.

Notice something else. You are very likely to be in a better mood than you've ever been in when planning feedback conversations. By thinking *positively* and in the *future* (vs. starting negatively and in the past), you are actively rewiring your brain to think of feedback as good for employees and good for you. You are associating feedback with guiding and helping people and—dare we say?—work-place happiness.

EVERYDAY-FEEDBACK TOOL:
Vision of highest good

	Notes
For whole team: Describe a scenario of wildly positive success 9–12 months in the future.	_____ _____ _____ _____ _____ _____ _____ _____
For individual employees: Describe each team member doing wonderful work 9–12 months in the future.	1. _____ _____ 2. _____ _____ 3. _____ _____ 4. _____ _____ 5. _____ _____ 6. _____ _____ 7. _____ _____ 8. _____ _____

EVERYDAY-FEEDBACK TOOL:
High-priority feedback chunks

Individual	Feedback Notes
Name	1. _____ _____ _____ 2. _____ _____ _____
Name	1. _____ _____ _____ 2. _____ _____ _____
Name	1. _____ _____ _____ 2. _____ _____ _____

CHAPTER 9

Step 3: Use COIN Phrases for Each Person

Now that you've thought about what you would love for your team to accomplish in the not-so-distant future, you're ready to meet with each player. As you prepare for your first round of individual feedback meetings, you may wonder what you are going to say. The COIN Feedback Method (figure 9.1) is an easy-to-remember template you can use for your first round of feedback conversations and for the

Connection to the person's goals and interests

Observations that are specific

Impact on the business

Next Steps: suggest, discuss, and agree upon

Figure 9.1. The COIN model

many more you'll have with each team member throughout the year. COIN will fit your situation, whether you're giving positive feedback or suggesting improvement. COIN takes the sting out of feedback because it links your feedback to what the employees want and to what the business needs. There is no room for personal attack or irrelevant comments.

COIN Feedback Method

The COIN model covers the four essential topics you need for great feedback:

C is for Connection

Connection means finding common ground with each individual and linking it to the feedback situation. First you should acknowledge something they want. Because personal wants vary widely among your team, you'll have to customize what you refer to. Here are some examples:

- becoming a group leader
- collaborating more with other functions
- developing greater responsibilities with customers
- mastering a new skill or responsibility
- improving upon past performance

Then connect them to a situation where you observed their work and how it relates to their goal or interest: "We've talked about your goal to be a project leader, and I wanted to go over your leadership of our team's progress meeting last week." It can be very simple: "Let's look at the brochure you just finished. I know you targeted it for new business." Still another might be "You've been targeting improved response time with customers, and I noticed . . ."

If you are discussing a feedback matter immediately after a meeting you both attended, connection probably already exists, as you're both interested in reviewing how it went. The context is right there, as you two have shared the experience. Perhaps you're even thinking similar thoughts as you leave the same meeting. However, if the feedback topic is something from the past or it's about something that might be confusing in terms of where and when, you need to spend a little more time setting it up. Try saying something like "Remember a few weeks ago how we handled these customers who wanted deep discounts? Now we are going to be dealing with them again, so I wanted to share some feedback that may help you with them."

When connection is missing, people become confused; they're not thinking about the topic you are talking about at that moment, and they're not sure why they should care. So, err on the side of providing more connection and context versus jumping into the topic cold.

O is for Observations

Observations are your descriptions of their work behavior. Make sure that your observations are specific and accurate. Avoid vague generalizations that will make the person feel confused or, worse, accused. At the same time, keep it quick, accurate, and to the point. Here are some examples:

- "You delivered that report three days early."
- "I noticed that you've not met with the group in the last two weeks, and we're going live next Friday."
- "You took extra time from your busy schedule to visit with the clients and show them around town."
- "Our new people are asking for help on this process, and you are sending them to Sandy."

Notice how these statements are factual rather than evaluative statements.

I is for Impact on business

Impact comments are results based, and can be positive, negative, or a mixture of the two.

- "Those two customers you targeted are doubling their business with us."
- "No decisions have been made, because the customers haven't received the information."
- "The client signed on for another year because they especially like working with you."
- "This delay caused another group to fall behind, resulting in lost revenue in this quarter."
- "Your focus on time management in that meeting helped the team make every decision needed for the launch!"

N is for Next Steps

Next Steps follow logically from your observations and impact statements. You will need to discuss, suggest, and agree upon the specific request you are making. Here, you are partnering with the team member to come up with an effective action or behavior change that will increase the business impact or continue the current impact, if it is positive. Feel free to begin the conversation with direct suggestions if you have helpful knowledge to share, but getting active involvement in this discussion is important because it increases the team member's commitment to the goal. Keep the feedback future-focused to build even more buy-in and, finally, clarify your expectations for what and when.

- "At my management meeting next month I'd like you to present your fact-filled report so you can provide the details you've mastered so well."
- "It will be good for you to practice slowing down with new

people. You mentioned George as a mentor. Can you work with him to come up with a special approach for them?"

- "Spending 100 percent of your time on this over the next three days is a great idea in order to focus on getting the project caught up."
- "I like your idea of an online tool to help other agents. This will prevent the mistakes. When can this be ready?"

When you link the next steps to solutions that will visibly improve results for the employee and for you, your feedback loops will move you forward. You have linked information about performance to current results, and the two of you are proposing an adjustment that will reap improvements.

EXAMPLE OF POSITIVE FEEDBACK

Connection

"We set a goal of cutting out 30 percent of the cost of sales support. I know you are committed to making it happen."

Observations

"I tracked the results and found that you and your team streamlined it even further: You've cut out more than 40 percent of the cost per customer!"

Impact

"This freed up our budget to focus on sales-rep compensation more in line with what you guys are contributing. That will improve morale."

Next Steps

"Please outline the key steps you took in leading the streamlining effort, and present it at our regional meeting. I think you'd be a great mentor to help the other groups improve."

EXAMPLE OF CORRECTIVE FEEDBACK

Connection

"I know your goal is to increase your impact with our customers by empathizing with their problems. You were concerned that they seem so stressed when they call."

Observations

"I've noticed this week that you seemed rushed when you talked to customers. When they approached your desk, you were looking at your screen and didn't make eye contact. Yesterday, Connie, a customer, called and said she felt you didn't care about her issue."

Impact

"The impact of this is that when the customer doesn't feel heard, we can't easily diagnose or address their needs."

Next Steps

"How do you think you can get a different response from people like Connie? OK, let's set up times to practice together your eye contact and mirroring of what the customer says. Then we'll review how this is working for you in another week."

Creating COIN scripts for everyone in your team results in a huge win because it creates learning relationships and stimulates everyone's desire for more feedback in your organization. A COIN conversation begs for follow-up, so you are opening a long-term dialogue and relationship with each employee.

COIN encourages you to spin your feedback loops faster within your team. You are providing the specific information the team members need in order to adjust. This will create an exponentially beneficial effect as you exchange feedback with every one of your team members and they, in turn, will offer feedback to you. (See next chapter, "Step 4: Ask for Feedback in Return and Adjust Big.") If you and they take it seriously, you will be demonstrating learning and change together.

Speed it up

When you are first broaching feedback conversations, you need to make sure to cover all four COIN topics thoroughly. Otherwise, people don't know where this sudden feedback is coming from. After those first few conversations, you can speed it up. Especially if you're following up or fine-tuning a particular feedback area—like time management or customer service—you will have already made the connection, and much of the impact will be evident to the feedback receiver as well. The O and N sections will always be new and different, however, so put emphasis there. Here are some examples of COIN used for your third or fourth conversation:

- "You've been getting high ratings in customer service, and this is drawing repeat sales. Keep it up, and let's share your new methods with the whole team!"
- "For the China launch, we still don't have data about why it hasn't picked up, so we still don't have a plan in place. Can you gather the data this week and call the group together?"

Create feedback scripts using the COIN template

Now is a good time to create scripts for each person on your team. You will need:

- your notes from the visioning you did in the last chapter
- a COIN planning worksheet (available at the end of the chapter

or downloadable from www.everydayfeedback.com) for each person on your team

For the first person on your agenda, review what you envisioned for them and what feedback area would most impact your team's result. (By the way, for your first script, remember to choose someone on your team you find easy to talk to, rather than someone who resists feedback, so you have a positive experience.)

Now go through the four COIN topics, starting with Connection. Jot down some phrases you can use to offer effective feedback to that person. Go through Observations, Impact, and Next Steps. You will notice that this flows easily and logically for most or all of your people. If you get bogged down, remember to prioritize the feedback items that, if improved, will have the greatest impact on the team's goals.

If you think that filling out these forms is too time consuming, realize that this is just a learning exercise so you can kick-start feedback. Later, you will do these steps mentally and in real time, as you naturally offer feedback that people can use.

EVERYDAY-FEEDBACK TOOL:
COIN planning worksheet for each employee

Instructions: Record a script for how to give feedback to this person.

Name: _____

Connection to the person's goals and interests	Observations that are specific
Impact on work results	**Next Steps:** suggest, discuss, and agree upon

CHAPTER 10

Step 4: Ask for Feedback in Return and Adjust Big

Once you start giving feedback on a regular basis you will start getting it, too. It's a natural human reaction that your employees will have advice for you when you suggest that they can do something better. To make it easier for you, seeking feedback yourself is built into the everyday-feedback process. After you've provided COIN feedback and agreed on next steps, you will be asking them how you can better support them in accomplishing their goals.

When you first ask for feedback from your employees about how you can do a better job at leading them, they may seem a little surprised and confused. But they will have a mental list ready.

Why is asking for two-way feedback so important?

When you ask people to do things differently, you are starting a whole new *conversation* and a whole new *relationship*. Since you are their boss, your team members want you to have a role in any change they take on. Put yourself in their shoes: If your boss started giving you feedback about a challenging part of your job, wouldn't you have something to ask of your boss?

The fact that you are inviting two-way feedback puts you on a peer, or team-member, level with the other person involved. This equality sends a soothing signal to the employee's brain that you can be trusted in asking them to relate to you on a personal level. Stirring up feelings of equality and camaraderie has an extremely positive effect on their openness to your feedback. When you evoke a feeling of connectedness, signaled by your own authentic emotions, both of you release the same positive brain chemicals that you would when you hang out with close friends, hold a baby, or fall in love. In contrast, one-way boss-to-subordinate feedback enforces the hierarchical relationship, and the employee feels more guarded and without control. Their fight-or-flight brain response, with its requisite surge of stress hormones shooting from the emotional brain, clouds their thinking abilities.

Chocolate

Asking for employees' feedback also conveys a sense of fairness and transparency, which has a very positive result. As David Rock explains in his article "Managing with the Brain in Mind," this sense of fairness lights up the same part of the brain as does eating chocolate.[37] Fostering the trust that comes from your willingness to sit down "on the same side of the table" and hear their feedback results in a huge, huge step toward establishing a learning relationship and motivating everyone to sign up for everyday feedback.

The other great thing about encouraging two-way feedback is that both you and your team member are now spinning your feedback loops faster and faster. As you make adjustments based on new information, you score exciting wins that prompt you to seek even more information. Both of you get hooked. This has an exponentially powerful effect. As you exchange feedback with each of your team members, everyone takes it seriously, it gets easier, and feedback gets more accurate and more timely.

Everyone has some feedback in mind

In the beginning stages of an everyday-feedback relationship, your team member is usually skeptical. Their feedback to you may not reassure you that their thinking is aligned with the business. The first comments they provide may seem a bit defensive or overly focused on logistics. Here are some examples:

EXAMPLES OF FEEDBACK FROM DIRECT REPORTS

At First

"OK, I see you want me to do this differently but you have never said so before. I was doing it the way I thought I should. I see now why you are saying this, but if I'm going to make this change, I need you to clarify some things. And actually, this new way of doing things means I can't do some of my other assignments in the same way either. So, I'll need you to help me go through my priorities [or my current process, or my competing demands, etc.] and figure out what and how to change."

Clearing the Way

"I need training on this process, and it's a bit frustrating because you've mentioned that there's no budget for training. Can you help us resolve this? Jerry and I would like to train each other on these new systems. Will you clear our time to do this?"

Make the Connections

"I see that this is very important to our customers, but our process doesn't allow it. I have some suggestions and would like your help in getting with players in other groups to fix this."

Empower Us

If you are patient and develop relationships with plenty of comfort and trust, you will begin to receive honest, solution-oriented comments like this: "When you don't involve us in those meetings and communications with the other group, I feel out of the loop and behind on the details. I'd like to start attending those weekly meetings with you."

Show positive changes yourself

Once you open the gates of feedback to flow toward you and once people get comfortable giving it, you will be the one getting the most feedback. Since your actions affect each individual you manage every day and you have now asked for feedback, there will be a lot of questions and suggestions directed your way. You may feel a bit overwhelmed at first, as individuals on your team are now expecting you to give them direction, information, encouragement, or training. This may proliferate in the first few weeks of your everyday-feedback campaign. Each team member is likely to need something from you, and you have to be ready to respond.

What's important is to show your sincerity in wanting to make a change and to show evidence of the change as quickly as possible. "It's not enough just to get feedback," writes Daniel Debow in *Fortune*. "Like working out, if you want to get in shape as a leader you have to do something about it."[38]

After receiving the feedback—especially if you're getting the same feedback from several people—acknowledge the item in a meeting and summarize some of the things you have heard; for example:

- "Thanks for your feedback about our ineffective scheduling process. Can a couple of you help me improve it?"
- "I know that several of you are asking for training; I'm working on making it happen."
- "I realize, from your great comments, that I allow myself to be distracted and interrupted when you're in my office, and I'd like to change that."

People are watching you more than you realize

Particularly after they have taken the risk to give you feedback, your team members will closely observe whether you have taken their feedback to heart. They will notice whether you are changing the way you have traditionally done things based on the specific topics of their feedback to you.

For example, if you continue to start meetings late after they provide their honest feedback about this practice, you are sending the message that their feedback does not matter. It's absolutely necessary for you to make a renewed effort to get the next meeting started on time and to make it efficient. Responding to their feedback accomplishes two goals. First, it improves results in your group; second, and most importantly, it is living proof that feedback is a positive practice! You are the role model on center stage. If you show everyone that you receive feedback well and can change your behavior as a result, you will earn a reputation for receptivity that, in turn, will encourage more people to give you constructive feedback.[39]

Feedback that is puzzling

Sometimes you will hear feedback that will make you scratch your head. Although you may not understand the message, it is critical to appreciate whatever the person is saying. If it's important to them, it's important that you listen. Give them your complete attention. Take notes. Ask for clarification and specifically ask what changes they'd like to see.

MARCELA

Marcela's direct report, Matt, told her that people in her group weren't being recognized enough. At first Marcela was surprised and a little irritated. She took a few deep breaths and then asked for clarification. Matt explained that although the team served the whole organization, they were kind of hidden. He also said that Marcela herself wasn't recognizing them enough. After thinking about it, she realized that he was probably right, but she had no clue as to what form of recognition people would most value. Marcela realized that recognition is a tricky issue because people value different forms of recognition. So, she took the time to visit with each team member about what kind of recognition they preferred. Then she implemented the most popular suggestions—and her team expressed great appreciation.

If you can't implement a change, be transparent

If you know that you can't make a change right away, let your team know right away. If you can make the change later, explain why there is a delay and when the change will occur. They will feel let down if you promise something and then don't end up doing it. Your inaction will feel like an insult and speak louder than any positive changes you are making.

Be honest about anything you don't think you can change right away or anything you can't change at all. The employee may make an unreasonable request without knowing it is unreasonable. For example, there may be an unpopular task that they wish you would assign on a rotation basis so that no one person does it often. If this approach is not workable, you need to explain why. You might say, for example, "Certain people must do that task because they are trained. This particular task can only be rotated among the people who are trained." As much as possible, offer a business rationale, be open to questions, and talk to them in a calm manner.

Compromise

If you can't make the change that employees request, try to compromise. You may find it very helpful to probe more deeply into the feedback they are bringing up and their experience of the problem. What will be the most satisfying solution for them, and what backup solutions can they suggest?

For instance, they may tell you that you're not accessible and you don't answer your email or phone when they need you. You may ask, "Can you describe the situations that were the worst for you, when you needed to reach me and I was unavailable?"

Acknowledge their feelings of frustration, and explain your situation in a nondefensive way: "I know there are times that I'm really inaccessible, because of business demands in the other location, but I can figure out ways to be more available than I am now. I'll set aside certain times of the day and make sure I look for urgent email."

Write a memo

Don't be shy about writing a memo. Feel free to write a memo to the team about a change that you want to make and how you are planning to go about it. In response to the feedback that you're inaccessible, you can say:

MEMO: THANKS FOR YOUR FEEDBACK

A couple of people have given me feedback that I am not as accessible as you need. You have helped me understand the impact of my unavailability. Thank you! I've been preoccupied with the new building project team, and for the next thirty days I'll continue to have less time than I usually do; this is unfortunate, because I would like to talk to you guys more often, too. I too am disappointed about this situation.

Because I know that accessibility is an important issue to your work, I have temporarily designated Terry as the go-to person for most issues. If there is something that's really personal that you want to email me about, I will make a new concerted effort to look at your email in the evenings and try to get back to you with at least a very short message telling you when I can talk to you or work with you on the issue. Again, thank you for your ongoing feedback; I am very excited about the feedback culture that we are creating in both directions, and I appreciate all of your great responses to our feedback meetings.

A big no-no: Dismissing, insulting, or being defensive

When you implement a feedback culture and request feedback yourself, you will likely have a couple of lively souls who want to use this opportunity to vent all of their complaints. They may even unleash critical remarks in a group meeting. While you may feel frustrated, don't overreact. Because you are trying to cultivate a beneficial feedback culture, it is absolutely essential that you *do not* insult, demean, or answer with a quick comeback. For every single comment, no matter how critical or challenging, it's important to preface any response with a thank-you for being courageous and sharing the feedback. There are a number of ways you can respond effectively, including: "That is an important concern, and in fact I would like to meet with you and Bobby about this because you guys are the most affected; can you stay after the meeting and we will set up a time to work on it together?" Then ask them more questions, such as:

- "What would be some effective ways to address that problem?"
- "Thanks for bringing that up. Hey, everyone, does this go into our high-priority meeting items for today, or shall we cover it another time?"

The important thing is to not censor their talking. Others who are more sensitive and less likely to make such critical remarks will be shut down if you overreact to a naysayer.

On the other hand, you don't want to allow the troublemaker to dominate your group's time or irritate or frustrate the other members of the team. You need a quick response—including a big thank-you for their input—that is not defensive. If you have a team member who is likely to make such remarks, plan ahead for how to deal with them productively! Prepare yourself to have a positive, nondefensive response so you can prevent them from hijacking the whole meeting.

Ongoing feedback for you

As you conduct weekly feedback conversations with everyone, you will be asking team members for their continuing feedback for you. Develop a positive philosophy toward their feedback, based on the following:

- showing gratefulness toward their feedback
- responding to their requests and regular status updates

- asking them for more feedback about your response and for their continuing support through feedback—keep it going!
- knowing that you are a role model for feedback; you are living proof that you can make positive adjustments and learn from the feedback loops your team is accelerating

EVERYDAY-FEEDBACK TOOL:
Receiving feedback "rehearsal"

1. Compose a few questions you'd like to ask to get team members' feedback and clarify what they are saying. Example: "What feedback do you have to help me lead the team forward on our strategy? When you say 'more communication about strategy,' what does that look like for you?"

_____

_____

_____

_____

2. What questions can you ask in meetings to elicit feedback and be a role model for feedback to happen? Example: "I want to hear from you guys about how I can better support each of you and the team as a whole. Specifically, what actions can I take that would improve our ability to excel?"

_____

_____

_____

_____

3. How can you show appreciation for the feedback people are providing?

_____

_____

_____

EVERYDAY-FEEDBACK TOOL:
Challenging feedback

Instructions: In the "Challenging Items" column, record three possible off-the-wall or difficult feedback items some of your group members might suggest to you individually or in a group setting. In the "Staying Open" column, compose one or two questions or comments you can make for each item to remain nondefensive and show you are listening. In the "Initial Responses" column, write your initial responses to their feedback.

Challenging Items	Staying Open	Initial Responses
Example: You need to increase our resources in the customer-support area by five more people. We're swamped over there.	Example: Tell me more about your idea. It's great that you're speaking up.	Example: You're right. We really need to address the overload you guys are experiencing. Can we explore this more? Then I'd like you to help me find a win-win solution for our team and for the company.
1.		
2.		
3.		

CHAPTER 11

Step 5: Create More Feedback Loops

Now that you have the first round of feedback under your belt and everyone lived through the experience, you're probably relieved and excited. Take a deep breath and acknowledge your courage and your commitment to great improvements for the team.

Right away you will notice that team members are making positive changes based on your feedback. Some of their new efforts may be awkward at first but you will see most employees giving it their best. Now's the time to jump in and acknowledge their new behavior and recognize that they've made a shift.

You'll notice people making some progress, but you may still see room for improvement. Make comments within a very short period of time—a day or two—after seeing the changes. First acknowledge that you have seen their positive changes, then add small suggestions, such as:

- "You may want to shift your efforts a little bit in this direction."
- "You're speaking up in meetings a lot more, which is great because you're such an expert. In fact, maybe you could speak up even more and give us more details."

For people who are clearly struggling, make sure to develop trust with them first, and then inquire about how it's going and offer help. Remember, now is not the time to criticize or demoralize anyone who's responding to your feedback.

Build on the momentum

Most of the people on your team have by now heard from others in the group that they too had a feedback meeting with you and that it was positive. Most of them are noticing your commitment to receiving feedback, your willingness to hear their suggestions about your leadership style, and your eagerness for more improvement ideas. Most of them have noticed that those individuals on the team who are outspoken have not been punished for expressing themselves.

A few days after you've started your rounds of feedback, acknowledge to everyone, in a meeting or in a memo, that you are very excited about the culture that is building in your team, that you see people using feedback well, and that you are receiving great, helpful suggestions. Remind them that you're trying to create a climate that promotes learning and everyone being OK with feedback; you're trying to build a culture where people aren't fearful of giving or receiving feedback; you're encouraging everyone to speak more honestly with one another; and you're looking forward to even more positive experiences with feedback.

Now you're on the road to a better relationship with each of your team members. The new relationship is based on honesty, frequent communication, and a genuine attitude of helping them. Your employees are already seeing you differently—as a coach who is developing them and an advocate and cheerleader who wants to see them win. Feedback is becoming a critical skill that builds your larger relationship with them as a coach and developer.

A few people are still skeptical

One or two on your team may still be Doubting Thomases, waiting for someone to be fired or reprimanded for sharing their honest ideas. Possibly there are a few people who are stuck in a fearful place, paranoid about "company speak," and actually very unaccustomed to having to think about what they want from you or the company. They may be making comments like these to their peers:

- "This feedback thing is going to blow over. Jay simply doesn't have time to talk to us all that often, and he doesn't really know what we're doing anyway."
- "I really liked it better with my boss staying out of my hair and me staying out of hers."

These individuals have probably experienced stress or trauma in other work settings and feel vulnerable about giving feedback to someone with power over them. Although you want to be sensitive to their needs, don't let these outliers hold you back. They too will see the value of the authentic feedback conversations and, eventually, join in the new culture after a few weeks or months of adjustment.

Get ready for your second round of feedback

It's suddenly time to initiate another round of feedback with each team member. Time may have whizzed by before you noticed exactly how great this new effort was going. Although you'll be setting up short meetings with everyone, you've probably already been in touch with most of them at least once even before the second round of scheduled meetings. Hopefully, you are feeling way more comfortable and so are they. Get ready for the fact that feedback isn't really such a big deal anymore. It's easier than you ever imagined, and it takes up way less time than you thought it would. Neither you nor your employees are as freaked out about the second conversation, and you will find you experience very little stress before having these conversations.

The only exception is when your everyday-feedback initiative has become the occasion for addressing poor performance by individuals you wished you had talked to more honestly ages ago. Pat yourself on the back now for confronting something important, for overcoming procrastination, and for moving toward positive change and resolution for everyone involved.

The challenge of keeping it up

Such a big change on the part of a busy leader—toward frequent, honest feedback—requires deliberate care and maintenance to prevent backsliding or confusion in the team. Although there will be logistical challenges that distract you from your everyday-feedback schedule, take solace in the fact that everyday feedback is more of a philosophy or new values system than it is an action plan. When you operate from everyday-feedback values, the actual feedback conversations can happen in a thirty-second hallway meeting.

The only backsliding you should worry about is when you get fuzzy in your values. Notice when you're lunching with a favorite employee and suppressing the need to give some feedback you think may dampen their spirit. Notice when you don't feel like picking up the phone to call a remote employee or use the COIN model to give positive feedback on an important win. These are the times when you want to recharge your commitment to that wonderful vision of the future.

How to speed up your feedback success

Here are some factors to consider when you want to move your everyday-feedback campaign along faster:

Speed factor #1: Honesty

When people are naturally honest with one another and become accustomed to exchanging feedback about how to improve things, the process goes much, much faster. For example, players on sports teams about to win a championship have no problem telling one another how to make a play better. An NFL player going to the playoffs is used to hearing honest feedback all the time from teammates who have an equal share in winning.

Likewise, in professional dance, the honest feedback that dancers exchange is called "notes." After a rehearsal, everyone in the dance troupe is asked, "What are your notes for this piece?" Go faster, more lighting, start farther from the left, and so on—honest comments tossed out with the full understanding that they're for the good of all. Interestingly, what went well—and should be repeated even if it was an accident—is just as important to call out as what didn't go well. A delay of a split second, a slightly exaggerated movement, and a facial expression can add up to a great performance.

Honest comments to sports-team and dance-troupe members are quick and part of the norm. The give and take of feedback is fast flowing when two conditions are met: a *clear common goal* and a *feeling of trust*. In your role, you can heighten both of these conditions by skillfully leading everyday feedback in your group.

I have timed people giving feedback to one another in top-level management teams. When everyone knows why they need to collaborate and there's a climate of trust, the team can brainstorm more than thirty candid feedback comments to each person—a mixture of positives and improvement items—in ten minutes or less per person. When there's no trust or no reason to work together, there's dead silence and a reluctance to say anything to anyone, good or bad.

Honesty equals speed

When a manager struggles, at performance-review time, to come up with two positives and two improvement needs per employee, the preparation time for each review can take hours. So, speed it up by reminding your brain that feedback is helping people and that it's one of the most effective things you can do as a leader. Set up a positive climate that your employees will pick up on. Great feedback can be exchanged in two minutes or less once there is familiarity and comfort with the process. Familiarity comes from frequency and a track record of helpfulness. Consider how long the following exchange would take:

> **Manager:** Very productive meeting you led, Kelly. Kept 'em on time and got their decisions. Next time we will need to get the folks from Western Division talking. They were looking disengaged by the end of the meeting. What do you think?
>
> **Kelly:** Yeah, thanks. I need to get more background on Western Division—will you meet with me and go over the history there?
>
> **Manager:** Yes, tomorrow. Let's come up with some questions you can ask them.

When you're working with someone you trust in a shared endeavor, feedback flows smoothly and doesn't feel personal. Feedback just feels like helpful information, like a compass indicating east or west. It's a navigation system, not a grade on their report card.

Speed factor #2: Prioritize

When you think you have to make an exhaustive list of everything an employee is doing well or poorly, it's overwhelming for both parties and it defeats the purpose of feedback to improve performance. There are usually one or two improvement areas that an employee can act on to create a greater turnaround in performance. When those areas are improved, you can go on to another area for the employee to focus on. You will probably need to remain on the same priorities for a while, as your employee will need both encouragement and more guidance on those one or two subjects.

Take one chunk at a time. If you're focusing an employee on better interpersonal communication with customers, you can prioritize asking more questions first. Once they're doing that consistently, you can help them come up with more probing questions that build on the customer's responses to earlier questions. Over time, you may need to go through a lot of feedback loops on one particular topic, but they will happen more quickly and effortlessly.

Speed factor #3: Superfrequent feedback

The more often you initiate feedback, the more comfortable your employee will be and, in turn, each feedback conversation can be short, sweet, expected, and easy to act on.

Speed factor #4: Staying future-focused to prevent defensiveness

If you offer helpful suggestions that the employee can see as relevant to their future success, and ask for their ideas for how to improve performance, you will have a better chance for avoiding defensiveness. The trick is to convert the learning from your review of past behavior (as in the Observations and Impact parts of the COIN model) into how they can be effective in the future. As you help them plan their action steps for the future, revisit the Connection part of the COIN model and link it to their Next Steps. Acknowledge the individual's career interests or values, and tie their next steps to how they can realize their own aspirations. Some starter phrases that soak in for employees include:

- "To help the team stay on track at the next meeting . . ."
- "For even better service the next time you meet with that customer . . ."
- "As you serve as leader for the new project we're launching next week . . ."

All of these phrases tap into the employee's feelings of hope, future possibilities, and success and motivate them to implement the improvements you are looking for.

You are now well on your way to making everyday feedback a lifestyle! You've gotten started, seen some good results, and now are seriously considering how you can keep up the momentum and learn more about giving great feedback. If you keep up the continuous feedback loops with all of your people, you will make it into the elite top five percent category of leaders who give frequent, honest, and helpful feedback. Far from being leaders who are disliked or feared, these are the leaders most appreciated by their engaged team members.

EVERYDAY-FEEDBACK TOOL:
Review of first week of everyday feedback

---

1. What are you proud of?

---

2. What surprised you?

---

3. In going forward, what do you want to make sure to do during the next feedback loop?

4. What positive message can you send to the whole team about their involvement with everyday feedback?

_____

_____

5. What interesting feedback did you get and what one or two comments seemed the most helpful?

_____

_____

For the members of my team, what do I need to mention next time?	
Name	Notes

CHAPTER 12

Step 6: Become a Great Coach

You'll find that everyday feedback is bringing you into a closer relationship with each of your employees. When you give honest feedback that is truly intended to help people, you are viewed as trustworthy and transparent. With trust, the brain remains in a more relaxed state and there is less fear of a surprise attack. Your brain is more relaxed, too, as you have overcome your fear of inflicting pain on people. Employees know that if you have a problem with something they are doing, you will let them know right away. When you, in turn, welcome feedback from team members, and respond by making adjustments in your own behavior, they see you as open to their ideas and truly a partner in their well-being.

Your employees now see you as someone on their side, someone who is there to offer helpful information for building their career. They feel a sense of pride in mastering new skills as you mentor them with tips and suggestions that you have learned throughout your career. You have begun to create a positive culture of better employee engagement and higher retention of talented employees. You have now expanded into the role of *coach*. The special coaching relationship is possible with every employee, but it must be tailored to the needs, personal styles, and belief systems of the individuals that you are coaching.

Coaching is a potent way to increase the resource base of your company and truly empower your employees to take on the business of achieving your team's goals.

Is feedback the same as coaching?

While feedback is one essential skill of coaching, a great coach draws on even more skills to address a wider spectrum of human development. While feedback is information that the other person can use to improve results, coaching is the process of guiding the person—through questions, encouragement, and feedback—to solve their own problems and achieve goals they're committed to.

Coaching takes less energy

The good news about coaching is that once you learn and practice great coaching, it actually requires *less* energy, and it results in less time feeling drained and exhausted than almost any other method of managing others. The bad news is that effective coaching often involves *unlearning* old ways of managing, leading, and coordinating the work of individuals. Coaching is deceptively simple, but it often means letting go of the old habits and behaviors that leave others in a more dependent role.

Outlined in figure 12.1 are six steps that lead you through effective coaching and into delivering powerful results to the organization and to empowered employees. Many of the skills necessary for effective coaching call on you to adjust your language and nonverbal communication to get in sync with the person you are coaching. Great coaching requires courage, but if you've truly launched honest feedback conversations, you've already shown the requisite courage. Coaching is largely an expression of *empathy* so that you can draw out the coachee's ability and motivation to solve their own problem.

The coaching cycle

Figure 12.1 shows a simple process for dealing with almost any kind of goal or problem that might come up in a coaching experience. Notice how it resembles the feedback loop you've come to know and utilize.

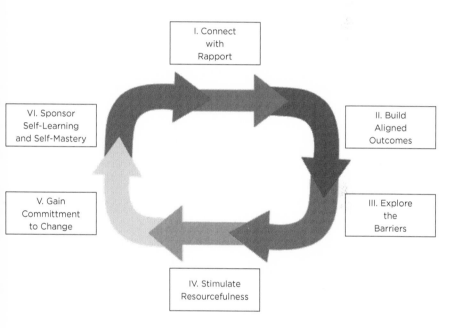

Figure 12.1. The coaching cycle

Let's take a look at each of these steps and see what they mean.

I. Connect with rapport

This will be easy for you if you've been successfully practicing everyday feedback. Indicating a relationship of mutual trust or emotional affinity, "rapport" stems from the old French verb *raporter*, which literally means to carry something back. This reflects the mutuality of the relationship: What one person sends out, the other sends back. The two of you share similar values, beliefs, or feelings. Eye contact and responsive facial gestures are indicators of good rapport.

When you go to any meeting or meet a new person, you may chat about nonbusiness issues, ask questions about their interests, or comment on sports, tablet computers, or other topics that could develop a friendly bond between the two of you. In addition, you may "read" people to get a sense of whether they understand or agree with what you're saying. Based on reading their nonverbal responses, you may feel called upon to make a spontaneous remark or nonverbal gesture that relaxes them or stimulates their interest. When based on an accurate understanding of the other's signals, you are demonstrating additional rapport skills that are great for excellent coaching.

Empathy

When you think of the people who are excellent coaches, you probably imagine people who seem to really listen and understand your unique interests and needs. This is the heart of rapport building. When someone is in rapport with you, they really are sensing the world in the way that you are sensing it; therefore, they understand the world similarly. When you're out of rapport with someone, you get the feeling that they do not understand your thoughts or feelings and that they are more concerned with their own needs.

Subtle ways to build rapport

You may have never considered some great ways to build rapport. Great communicators use many of the following techniques:

Focused eye contact

While you don't want to make someone uncomfortable by staring them down, it's important to establish eye contact and sustain it a few seconds longer than you are used to doing it. Have you ever felt that someone was out of rapport with you because they simply weren't looking at you at all while you were talking? You may have had a colleague or customer who spent almost all the time looking away and it made you feel uncomfortable.

The normal cycle for most people is a few seconds of eye contact followed by looking away, a few more seconds of eye contact followed by looking away, and so on. Practice having your eye contact linger one, two, three, maybe even five seconds longer than normal and take note of the effectiveness on others. You can practice on family members and outside friends, as well as people in your organization.

Listening without interrupting

Listening without interruption is one of the greatest gifts you can give another person. The person being coached will become more and more comfortable expressing their own thoughts and feelings without fear that they will be shut down, interrupted, corrected, or unheard. The more you make it clear that you are not going to interrupt their flow of thoughts, the more relaxed they become and the easier it will be for them to share with you their true ways of seeing the world.

This may be frustrating for some of us who have become successful by our fast-paced, directive style. One way to relax and become less frustrated is through deep breathing from the diaphragm. Another is to completely focus on what the other person is saying with no rehearsal of an answer or a suggestion. Allow a few seconds after the person finishes a thought in order for them to continue without interruption. Finally, if necessary, count to five between their sentences to make sure you don't jump in with a quick retort.

Backtracking or paraphrasing

Backtracking is when you repeat some of the person's words to check for understanding and to show them that you heard what they said. Paraphrasing is similar, but involves changing their words into your own words. The difference between paraphrasing and backtracking is really interesting when it comes to rapport building because some people respond better to backtracking only while others respond well to either backtracking or paraphrasing. If you paraphrase and the person corrects what you said, then try direct backtracking. It may seem silly that you are parroting what they say, and you may fear they will be offended by this, but once you become experienced with it you'll see that people actually like to hear their own words repeated—your backtracking is music to their ears.

Matching voice and posture

Mirroring is a great technique, but if it's overdone it can seem artificial. It's easy to get the impression that it is simply a "monkey see, monkey do" game, but that's not the case. Matching or adopting similar characteristics of the other person's voice and posture is something that all of us do naturally when we're in rapport. When you are in deep rapport with another individual, your posture, breathing, and tone of voice begin to match the other's. Scientific studies of parents and babies, close friends, or even business colleagues who admire one another demonstrate this repeatedly with the use of videotape and breathing monitors.

This matching of behavior is not a copycat game. It's subtler than that. If you do it with a focus on being in tune or in sync with the other person, it can be extremely effective. If the person you're coaching talks very slowly, slow down your speech somewhat. Likewise, if they talk excitedly or gesture with their hands, modify your own voice and gestures, but not to a ridiculous degree.

Avoiding the urge to pull them on to your "map" too early or too often

This is one of those unlearning points and one of the hardest to overcome. It can crop up easily when you're trying to deliver feedback. The more empathetic we try to be, the more we want to share our own experiences with others. Jumping in too early by relating your own experience (that may or may not be similar) is often a turnoff.

Very often our "map" is actually different than the other person's, and when we start expressing things they don't feel, they feel the disconnect. You may hear an employee talk about a feeling that there's no room to advance in the company. If you jump in quickly with your own story about starting a job fifteen years ago when times were tougher and there were even fewer advancement possibilities, it may break your rapport with them. The other person may perceive that fifteen years ago, there were great opportunities in the business world, and that somehow the current climate is different—whether or not it's true. It's best to hear them out and really explore your employee's perceptions before providing your own background or experience with it.

Responsive facial expressions

Responsive facial expression is a rapport builder that comes naturally to most people. The only warning here is to folks who don't realize that they frown or avoid smiling much of the time. Ask your friends and colleagues whether you smile often or appear animated. You may not be aware that people—particularly people you're coaching—may be intimidated if you frown or don't show any expression when someone tells you about a problem or a concern. You may not seem open and available to them. If you usually refrain from head nodding and facial expressions, begin to practice. On the other extreme, too much facial animation can be distracting and disruptive to the person communicating with you.

Ask questions to clarify—don't assume

After listening, open-ended questioning is the best all-around communication technique. However, your questions must reflect real interest in what the person is saying. As soon as the person mentions a problem or issue that you recognize, avoid the temptation to jump in and assume that you understand what they're saying. Ask for examples that can help you deepen your understanding. Make sure you ask for details when vague words and phrases come up.

For instance, "communication" can really mean anything. If someone comments, "I don't feel that our team is communicating enough," ask what's missing and what would feel like better communication. You will likely need clarification, so it's best to avoid interjecting your own thoughts about the issue before you ask open-ended questions and hear their responses.

Reading body language for disagreement or confusion

An individual's facial expression or even posture may indicate confusion or disagreement with what you're saying. You might be fairly good at reading your boss's face for lack of approval. But it's also important to get as good at reading your team members' expressions and interpreting these correctly.

The way to practice is to take note of their facial expression when you know they agree with you or are happy about something. Also note their facial expression when you are certain they disagree or are confused by something. Then later when you see a confused expression, you will read it accurately and pause to clarify their confusion or misunderstanding. For instance, if you ask them to do something and they look confused, stop and ask: "Was that confusing? Can I explain that better?"

Modifying your approach

Modify how you communicate in order to send a more effective message. If you don't stop to clarify a point, you will distance yourself and create more misunderstanding. For example, if you continue to justify your behaviors, even after you realize that the other person has been upset, you will create a gap in rapport between the two of you. Facilitate better communication by pausing to ask them about their perceptions.

II. Build aligned outcomes

An outcome is a goal that the person you are coaching sets for the future. However, there are many different types of goals—some are aligned and others aren't. To be truly achievable, an outcome is best stated in terms of what the person can do and is in control of rather than what others do or are in control of. In other words, if the person you're coaching complains about coworkers, the lack of advancement in the company, or the myriad other forces that lie outside their control, they will be very frustrated if they're not able to change those circumstances. If you help them reframe their goal as an action or new way of thinking they can personally adopt, they are in control and in charge of making it reality.

Recognizing lack of control

If the person you are coaching suggests that the behavior of coworkers is a problem you should deal with, it's important to help them concentrate on their own actions or reactions. This is not to say that a manager should not address issues with coworkers or with the whole team if you also see these to be a problem. But, in coaching the individual, the only way to be effective is to help the individual become empowered to make changes themselves. This applies in all kinds of situations and outcomes you may be presented with. If someone feels stymied by their job, you might help them shift their focus to actions, training, preparation, or other initiatives that can enhance their role, rather than waiting for you or others to place them in a new position (unless, of course, that's a viable option).

You can best help the person reframe their desired outcome in terms of what they can actually achieve by simply asking, "Is this in your control?" "Is this something that you have the power to change?" "Can we restate the goal in terms of something you can control?" "Can you state that as something you will change versus what others need to change?"

Make the goal positive

Another condition of an aligned outcome is that it be stated positively. In other words, instead of saying something like "I want to stop getting so mad at my peer in the lab," you can help the person state it in terms of "I want to choose a better response when I feel frustrated with my coworkers." Or "I want to remain calm when other people make me feel stressed." In order to coach on building a positive outcome, you may simply ask, "Can we restate that in the positive?" "Is there a way to turn that around and have you choose a positive response in those situations?"

Alignment is ensuring that the goal or outcome is complementary with the goals of the organization and with the individual's personal goals. The person won't want to do something that is not really going to have a positive impact on the organization. As coach, you can help them reframe their goal in terms of something that is valuable to the organization.

Career alignment

However, if the goal is something that is very deeply felt by them and ultimately would take them away from contributing to the organization, your job is to draw out these values and thoughts so that they can set a goal that may lead them to quitting, if that is their heartfelt dream. For instance, the person may feel very frustrated by the job and they have gone through a number of steps to try to enhance their role. When both you and the individual have done everything possible to enhance the role and it's clear that they want an entirely different professional or career path, it would be helpful to help the individual express those strong desires and see the need to take steps toward realizing their dream.

Alignment with personal life

Usually alignment is very positive because it's easy to see that many of the solutions to their frustrations and even career needs are in sync with the needs of the organization. Another area of alignment might have to do with the person adopting a goal, such as finishing an MBA in one year on top of having new twin babies and leading a hectic project. You can help them explore the possible stressors involved and possible consequences. As a coach, you can ask questions such as "How will this affect your health?" and "How will this affect your family?" as you deal with the issue of how it's going to affect the work setting itself.

Workability of goal

Once the person understands the possible areas of alignment, they're usually quite cooperative in admitting that they need to consider other aspects of their goal. Finally, it's really important to make sure that the goal or outcome is the proper size. In other words, if the outcome is too large or grandiose, it will be difficult to achieve it in a timely fashion and feel good about it. You might help the person break down a too-large goal into workable chunks. Conversely, some individuals may have goals that are too narrow or specific, which will lead to frustration when they can't be achieved exactly in the desired form. An example would be someone who wants a very specific job description as the next step in their career. If it's too narrow, the goal may not be in reach and is therefore out of their control. As you can see, there are quite a few details to consider when helping someone achieve a goal. As you help them build an aligned outcome, you will be halfway to helping them achieve something meaningful.

III. Explore the barriers

Now you're ready to help them understand what is needed to achieve their goals. Before jumping right into a game plan, help them understand barriers that may have prevented them from achieving their goal so far. These barriers may fall into the following categories: knowledge gap, skill gap, and belief gap.

It's usually beliefs that block

It's interesting to note that while knowledge and skill gaps can indeed be barriers to people achieving their goals, what really hampers them are their long-established beliefs about themselves or about the world. These beliefs or attitudes may hinder their ability to acquire the knowledge or skills they need. For example, if an individual believes that they are bad at math and it's tough for them to learn financial practices, then they will have trouble asking others what kind of courses or skills they need to gain more financial capabilities. It may come to them as "I just don't know what courses to take" or "I can't master the financial skills needed for the job." In another knowledge area, they may present the problem as a kind of simple logistical hurdle, like "I don't know who to talk to," when it may really boil down to a negative or incorrect belief that has hampered them in getting the right information. Coaches, as positive outside influences, can most effectively explore *all* of these levels of barriers. Your role as coach can be very fruitfully applied to helping people explore their beliefs or misconceptions about their own capabilities and shift to a more positive outlook.

Empowering questions

To ask empowering questions effectively requires a lot of listening, a lot of patience, and a lot of probing questions. Your first question might be "What do you think is stopping you from achieving this outcome?" Then, you can follow up with these questions:

- "What are your beliefs about this situation?"
- "Where are these 'shoulds' and 'musts' coming from?"
- "Why has this worked or not worked?"
- "Can you tell me a story about when you tried to achieve this outcome?"
- "What was the hardest step for you?"
- "What would be possible if you had a different belief about your ability in this area?"
- "What would happen if you had a different belief about what others 'should' do?"
- "What else can you do to achieve this outcome?"

People often have rigid rules for themselves or others that are accompanied by "should," "must," or "have to." As a coach, it's your job to help them see how they may be hindering their own progress by ascribing their rigid rules to themselves or other people, thus getting in the way of achieving positive results. This may seem to require a great deal of skill on your part, but it is mostly a listening and questioning process that you will get better at over time. This is a moment in the coaching relationship when too much advice from you can get in the way of people realizing what their own barriers to success are.

Your stories

It's OK at this point to share a few stories about how you or others have explored and clarified barriers. However, make sure your words are not too prescriptive, such as "Therefore, you need to go do this, too." You may want to use the phrases "This may or may not be helpful to you, so here's another idea" or "A barrier that someone else had a few years ago was . . ." If they seem to reject the example or idea, quickly go back to open-ended questioning to find out how they feel about the situation. Very often, just listening to them voice their perceived barriers will help them gain a new insight about how they approach or attack it in a new way.

Give feedback

This is the time to provide the helpful performance-based feedback that you have become so comfortable giving. True coaching involves continued rapport and trust, and your accomplishments with giving feedback will fit in nicely. Now that you've gotten them to articulate an outcome for something they really want to do or achieve, your feedback will be well received because it will be focused on what's holding them back from achieving their goal.

IV. Stimulate resourcefulness

Here's where the two of you can come up with all kinds of alternatives, especially emphasizing alternatives generated by the person you're coaching. You may also want to include positive feedback at this point, reminding them of ways they've handled other situations positively in the past and reinforcing how their abilities will help them address the goal or outcome. This step may require several discussions to be fully explored. Here are some useful questions:

- "What are some things you could do to move forward on this?"
- "What are some ways to get past these barriers?"
- "Who would be helpful to you in learning about solutions or skills you need?"
- "What are some things you could work on in the next few weeks to make progress on this outcome?"
- "If you looked at this issue in a completely different way, what would be a 'crazy' solution?"
- "What are you willing to challenge yourself to do in order to really achieve this outcome?"

If you have suggestions, you can offer them as part of the brainstorming session rather than as a one-way teaching approach.

V. Gain commitment to change

You need an action plan, but you need one that comes with full commitment. A solution or exciting new goal can slip away if the person you are coaching hasn't brought their attention to the steps they will need to take. They can avoid sabotaging themselves if you explore their emotional commitment to the plan. Start with what the person is going to do when they walk out of your office or conference room today. What specifically are they going to be doing differently? How will they track their progress and get more assistance from you and others? Having a brilliant problem-solving session may be very helpful, but if they are ill prepared to make the changes they identified, they will remain stuck.

It's important that you, as the coach, take on the role of leading the individual to commit to making one or more specific steps. If the action plan involves a tough conversation with one or more people, it's helpful if you role-play or rehearse the approach they will be taking. Be patient as you suggest adjustments in their script for talking with key influencers. Phrase a suggestion as "An approach you may want to consider for saying that is . . ." or "A helpful approach may be . . ." Compliment the person on the parts of their method that work most effectively.

VI. Sponsor self-learning and self-mastery

The whole coaching cycle supports self-mastery. It's the mind-set you are bringing to how you work with your team members.

It may be hard to really understand or appreciate just how influential you are as a coach in this person's life. If you are the individual's manager, every word you say, every hint about the future, and every cryptic comment about upper management has a big impact. Individuals hearing you make these statements will make decisions based on your views, so use your influence wisely! It's important to maintain your bond of rapport and keep directing them to reflect on their own goals, decisions, accomplishments, and new insights. Encourage them to seek feedback information everywhere and to learn from feedback loops they set up on their own.

Authentic feedback has enabled you to have learning conversations with everyone. Now, as the coach, you will energize yourself, each individual you manage, and your whole team toward business and personal mastery.

EVERYDAY-FEEDBACK TOOL:
Assess your coaching capabilities

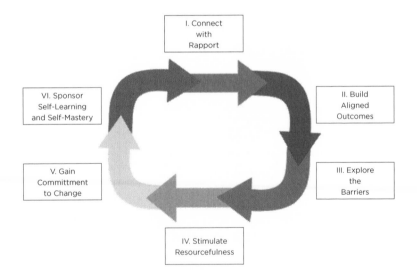

Instructions: Rate yourself on a scale of 1–3 on each coaching capability—the higher the number, the higher the capability.

		Total
1. Connect with rapport.		
• I use eye contact, facial expressions, and other nonverbal cues to encourage and empathize.	—	
• I use language that aligns with the other person's style, pace, and emotional state.	—	
2. Build aligned outcomes.		
• I use questions skillfully to understand a person's goals and priorities.	—	
• I advise the person to set meaningful goals or outcomes.	—	
3. Explore the barriers.		
• I explore barriers and engage the person to anticipate possible barriers.	—	
• I probe to help the person dig for emotional as well as logistical barriers.	—	
4. Stimulate resourcefulness.		
• I guide the person to see a range of solutions.	—	
• I avoid solving the problem for the other person.	—	
5. Gain commitment to change.		
• I help the person break down solutions into workable action.	—	
• I help the person with a reality check regarding conflicting priorities.	—	
6. Sponsor self-learning and self-mastery.		
• I provide positive reinforcement for learning demonstrated on the job.	—	
• I engage the person to reflect on feelings about self-mastery.	—	
Based on the areas you'd like to develop more, what learning actions are important to commit to now?		
_____		
_____		
_____		
_____		

PART FOUR

FASTER FEEDBACK
LOOPS TO
ACCELERATE THE
WHOLE COMPANY

CHAPTER 13

Feedback in the Top Leadership Team

Up to this point, every aspect of feedback we've been talking about applies to the top leaders of any organization—only even more so.

Executive leaders have the most control over the speed of feedback loops

If you are a VP, CEO, or anyone who reports to the CEO, your everyday-feedback behavior has a huge microphone on it—sending loud, clear signals throughout the company. If you talk about the importance of feedback, it will be noticed. And if you give everyday feedback yourself, it will always be heard.

Whether your organization's feedback efforts are going well or poorly, you are already influencing everyone's attitudes about feedback. Lower-level managers are probably having conversations about you like these:

- "The CFO never gives feedback to his management team, so I don't need to spend much time giving it to my team, either."

- "Wow, our CIO is great at giving feedback to everyone on our management team. I had to get used to this feedback culture because it's so different than where I came from. Here I'm expected to sit down with my people on a weekly basis."
- "Our CEO is the most conflict averse person I've worked with. He doesn't encourage anyone to exchange feedback."
- "The only feedback those guys get is when the executive director wants to fire someone. It happens without any warning, and the person just disappears in the night."
- "Our CEO is taking the lead in getting every manager to develop their people more via feedback and coaching. Now each of us is having these conversations with our team members."

Some executives in knowledge-intensive industries see the need

eBay CEO John Donahoe encourages everyone in the company to embrace an "open, honest, and direct" style of communication. High-tech giants Intel and Microsoft have been longtime promoters of honest feedback in all decisions and expect it in all meetings—even to the point of promoting "constructive confrontation."

Bridgewater, the world's top hedge fund, is led by CEO Ray Dalio, who's built a culture that enforces radical honesty. Every single employee is expected to provide input openly in every single conversation or meeting. People are given positive reinforcement for contributing honest feedback, and they are considered a cultural mismatch if they avoid feedback. Although the Bridgewater culture of "extreme feedback" is viewed outside the company as controversial, feedback is considered by leaders there as key to better decisions and excellent company performance.

Social media giants Twitter and Facebook have leaders who preach and practice frequent feedback and have even set clear expectations for the pace of feedback. Twitter expects everyone to exchange five minutes of feedback immediately after meetings. Twitter leaders at all levels are expected to have a short, weekly feedback-and-development meeting with each employee.

The difference an everyday-feedback culture makes

All of this feedback infuses a company's culture with fast-flowing information, better results, and a sense of excitement. Team members have their ears perked for new information. Employees are hearing the truth in real time and wasting less time speculating on what their bosses and colleagues think.

Have you noticed that when someone shares an honest opinion about a controversial issue, everyone in the room suddenly sits up straight, fully awake and tuned into the speaker? Feedback unleashes energy as it destroys the weighty drag that comes from uncertainty and conflicts that lie under the surface.

You can promote transparency without creating toxic conflict. You can dramatically accelerate your company's virtuous feedback loops by doing feedback yourself and by expressing its value—essentially teaching the whole organization through your everyday-feedback values. A top leader must only do two things to make everyday feedback happen:

1. Give everyday feedback yourself.
2. Make it a company value.

Follow the Six Steps to Everyday Feedback outlined in this book to do it yourself. The way to make it a company value is to be a passionate evangelist about feedback and to hold leaders accountable for doing it. And think about the strategic value of everyday feedback in your particular office environment. Is it just another management tool, or is it a truly revolutionary way to speed up success?

Think about the business goals and plans you are most focused on. Are they product innovation, operational improvements, service issues, talent development, global strategy, and disruptive technologies? How important is it for smarter thinking and problem solving to be brought to bear on these topics? How helpful would it be to accelerate your company's feedback loops in order to increase the success of your business goals? Do you see the return on investment in human feedback exchanged between every leader and every employee?

If you don't think of everyday feedback as a giant innovation, then it's not worth your effort to implement it. Without a passionate commitment to faster feedback, you will experience uneasiness with the new level of honesty, and team members will roll their eyes as they see feedback abandoned in a few weeks, just as they predicted. But if you can see that everyday feedback will give you a true competitive advantage, then it is worth your time and energy and you will be able to lead your company to the positive horizon you see clearly ahead.

Feedback barriers common in executive teams

Of course there are some challenges to giving everyday feedback in the executive team.

Challenge #1: You carefully selected and hired expensive, talented leaders to run big groups within your company and you don't want to micromanage them.

These leaders are high-initiative, independent thinkers who bring a wealth of functional expertise. You want them to lead large parts of your business. Since you're not supervising their day-to-day activities and you expect them to operate independently, you may be hands off and thus not offer feedback. You may think that the regularly reported business metrics are enough and that they can see what's needed on their own.

Marshall Goldsmith points out, "Executives avoid coaching because they are afraid of alienating their direct reports. In general, the higher people rank in organizational hierarchy, the more expensive they are to replace."[40] But this is not a good rule of thumb. Everyone benefits from an ongoing feedback and coaching conversations with their manager. "Hands off" is simply off base.

Be the culture connector

While there is virtue in high-level managers being able to operate autonomously and to focus on what they're held accountable for, they still need you to coach them. You are the *culture connector*. No one group or function stands alone. They need your guidance to connect their part of the business to the larger whole—to the values, to the culture, to the heart and soul of your company. If you are the CEO, you are the chief culture officer for the whole company, and your coaching will help them align their communication, their decisions, and their evolving belief systems with your own and with those of other top leaders. If you are not the CEO of the company, but are the top leader of a business unit or function, you are the "CEO" of your group; the same reasons apply as to why you need to provide feedback and coaching to your management team.

Use positive feedback to spread best practices

You are the top disseminator of your company's best practices. You are best positioned to observe what your leaders are doing well and to suggest some of these good ideas to other leaders and groups. A focus on everyday feedback will yield many more great ideas and solutions than a CEO's typical reports and meetings. Your leaders will feel appreciated. You will be sending a message about what is important, and positive results will increase. Even more important, these leaders you manage will mimic your feedback behavior in their teams, and it will just keep expanding from there.

You'll readily engage in a constructive dialogue with your leaders when problems arise. When you see or hear something that concerns you, the relationships with each of your team members, based on everyday feedback, make it easier to go to them personally and share an open dialogue about what's going on and how to address it. Even when serious problems arise, because of the trust you have established, both of you are less likely to experience a defensive stress response, even when serious problems arise.

Rather than relying on rumors about problems from third parties, you will be receiving quicker and more accurate information directly from your management team members, who have become comfortable asking for your help. If you explore the circumstances and find solutions collaboratively, your team members will feel deep appreciation for your guidance. They will be motivated to address problems even earlier next time and to trust you to continue empowering them.

Challenge #2: You're busy, traveling frequently, and not so accessible

While this is completely understandable, think of everyday feedback as a time-saving key to faster conversations. You can find five- to ten-minute time periods for communicating with each of your direct reports at least once a week, and anytime there are concerns. If you help them get clearer on the company's shared goals and values, they become more, not less, capable of running their part of the business independently. This investment of a few minutes per week talking to each of your direct reports will save you hours on problems and issues that will rob you of much more time.

The other executives on your team are probably not giving adequate feedback to their direct reports, who are clamoring for it. Since 95 percent of managers everywhere are failing to give adequate feedback (that statistic is even higher for top executives), it's clear that attention must be focused on leading the feedback effort. You are the only one who can really ensure that feedback happens consistently. If you believe in feedback and in developing people, you must spend time with your leadership team to ensure that all of them exchange feedback with their team members. You can insist on this by giving them feedback on their feedback.

Challenge #3: Can everyday feedback help correct executive hiring mistakes?

Here's an example of too little feedback in the executive suite:

EXECUTIVE CHURN AT ANCHOR

Timothy is the CEO of the Anchor Company, an innovative product developer in the electronics industry. Anchor has faced difficult challenges lately with new competitors on the scene. Throughout Anchor's history, they have gone outside to recruit qualified candidates for all of their executive roles, and they have high standards for which candidate they select. Anchor pays higher than the industry average.

However, Anchor has made a number of hiring mistakes along the way. After two or three years, they now realize that a person they chose isn't performing as well as they wanted, and they want to release him from the company. The typical mode of firing people was "taking them out" by simply offering them a large severance package in exchange for an agreement not to sue for wrongful termination. Someone would have a five-minute conversation with them to say, "It just isn't working." After the executive signed the severance agreement and disappeared "in the night," it was announced that the person had resigned from the company. No prior feedback had been given to clue them in that their work was unsatisfactory, even though the executive team had had whispered conversations beyond earshot of the person who was about to be fired.

In this organization, there was no everyday feedback and often no annual performance review for the executive team. This mode of taking out leaders created fear in the company. People knew that there would be no warning if their work was not acceptable and worried that they would be fired next, creating a culture in which learning was slow and feedback conversations were unavailable to help people improve.

Such a scenario impairs organizational improvement. The fearful attitude of executives trickles down to all levels. Companies like Anchor become known among employees as a culture where they are not coached or developed. If a leader is struggling, they are simply replaced with another candidate.

There is so much waste—of resources, time, energy, and the emotional investment of the people who do the work. It's hard to believe that the root cause of such sudden drastic changes could be one person not wanting to talk honestly with someone he recently hired, but it's true.

Feedback is the remedy that will develop people at all levels—from executives to hourly team members. While it is true that a small percentage of the people you hire may not be a good match and will need to be separated at some point, there is much that can be done earlier on in the process to develop the person and make sure they are aligned with the company's goals. If they continue to be misaligned, then weekly feedback conversations will bring to the surface the person's refusal to focus on key goals. It's likely that the poor performer will leave of their own accord, realizing that they are not a good fit. Not only will this cost the company much less money than a severance-based "takeout," but it will also prevent the contagion of fear unleashed with frequent firings.

You've unleashed great things

Your everyday-feedback campaign will have a huge multiplier effect on results throughout the company because leaders at all levels will have a role model to follow and they will be far more motivated to work consistently and well. Every leader will be expected, as part of their performance goals, to engage in everyday feedback. Great things will happen.

All it takes is a motivated CEO and at least one other person in the executive leadership team to make everyday feedback a reality. Before actually kicking off a campaign for all managers, the executives should plan to test out the program among themselves. This will start with the CEO talking to each executive team member about the overall plan for giving people more information that will help them grow, learn, and achieve better results. After each team member receives feedback from the CEO and after the CEO receives feedback in return, the feedback loop can encompass the whole organization, following the Six Steps to Everyday Feedback at all levels.

What's really important is to know is that all eyes and ears will be focused on your executive team now and throughout the year. It's a make-or-break commitment that you'll be initiating.

How to make the commitment

Before committing to everyday feedback, executive team members must hash out the following:

- whether they feel that feedback is something they really want themselves
- whether they are willing to give and receive feedback from each of their direct reports (most or all of whom will be leaders themselves)
- whether they're willing to hold their direct reports accountable for giving and receiving feedback

A halfhearted effort to launch feedback is much worse than just having individual managers launch it in pockets of the organization. At least the managers in pockets who are launching feedback will be personally committed to doing it. If executives aren't willing to follow through on feedback they've announced with a splash, then a strong message will be sent throughout the organization that it's not really important.

Customizing the Six Steps to Everyday Feedback

Some of the steps outlined in earlier chapters of this book will need to be customized when the CEO introduces them in the executive team:

Step 1: Explain what you are doing

This is largely going to be the role of the CEO and at least one other cheerleader spreading the gospel of everyday feedback—the purpose of it and the need to make it a sustained effort. This step may be awkward at first because many organizations have had little or no feedback in the past. Initiating feedback is a big step, and there may be some fear and fight-or-flight reactions that are unleashed within members of the executive team. It is advisable to discuss the feedback initiative in at least three full meetings of the entire executive team and allow plenty of time for discussion, questions and answers, buy-in, and planning for implementation.

Announce the feedback initiative throughout the organization. Begin as soon as everybody has received at least one feedback meeting and has provided feedback to the CEO. You can announce the process while it's under way. Each person in the executive team can begin sharing the feedback with their teams. Ideally, each executive will share at least one learning goal they have committed to after receiving feedback. It will be supereffective if every member of the executive team actually demonstrates some progress on a key area addressed in their feedback.

Step 2: Look for the highest good

Envisioning the highest good for each member of the executive team simply means sharing positive visions you have for each function or group (e.g., product group, sales team, finance, etc.). So, in some ways, the visioning step may be even easier at the executive level because you are probably already doing it.

Step 3: Use COIN phrases for each person

Make sure that every executive receives COIN feedback on how effectively they give feedback. Gather observations by asking them what they are doing in their feedback meetings and by talking with their direct reports. This will be a key performance indicator for everyone in the top leadership team. If there are leaders who are good at giving feedback, the CEO should hold them up as role models.

Step 4: Ask for feedback in return and adjust big

This step is absolutely essential. Every single employee who knows about the feedback initiative will be noticing the behavior of the executives and whether they are taking it to heart.

Step 5: Create more feedback loops

Implementing more feedback loops is particularly important if there are reluctant executives in the group who are just going along with the CEO to comply with their boss's wishes. If there are areas where leaders are displaying negative attitudes, it's important for the CEO to have a conversation with them about why they're reluctant and to help them move forward.

Step 6: Become a Great Coach

While coaching conversations led by executives may happen less frequently than individuals on the team would like, they are very powerful when they do happen. Executives who take the time to explore goals, barriers, and solutions with each direct report are the most valued leaders of all.

A leader in an everyday-feedback environment can't solve everyone's problems, but they are passionate about their mission to speak their truth, be trustworthy, and promote those qualities in others.

The highest potential growth area for a leader walking the everyday-feedback journey is the growing willingness to be honest with others. James O'Toole and Warren Bennis summarized the value of honesty:

> Tell the truth. When followers are asked to rank what they need from their leaders, trustworthiness almost always tops the list. Leaders who are candid and predictable—they tell everyone the same thing and don't continually revise their stories—signal to followers that the rules of the game aren't changing and that decisions won't be made arbitrarily. Given that assurance, followers become more willing to stick their necks out, make an extra effort, and put them on the line to help their leaders achieve goals.[41]

One CEO—or another executive in the C-suite—who is willing to spread their passion for feedback can change a large company, turn around a business, and ignite employees' excitement about contributing to something great. Authentic feedback values leveraged by a person with a high level of influence can't be stopped!

EVERYDAY-FEEDBACK TOOL:
Six Steps to Everyday Feedback

Instructions: For the Six Steps to Everyday Feedback listed in the left column, record the specific actions you plan to take for making this work in the top executive team.

Six Steps to Everyday Feedback	Special Actions
Step 1: Explain what you are doing	*Example: Clarify with the group exactly how often we'll do it and the format we'll use.*
Step 2: Look for the highest good	*Example: I'll set a feedback priority for each member of my team related to the key strategy for their whole group.*
Step 3: Use COIN phrases for each person	*Example: As CEO, I'll use COIN to prepare feedback, starting from scratch and not looking at past performance review.*
Step 4: Ask for feedback in return and adjust big	*Example: After each team member gives me some feedback in initial meetings, I'll summarize all of the comments for the larger group.*
Step 5: Create more feedback loops	*Example: I'll ask each team member to initiate meetings with me.*
Step 6: Become a great coach	*Example: Meetings will be one to two hours each, preferably off-site, to explore future goals.*

CHAPTER 14

Feedback Everywhere in the Organization

What if you're not an executive in a large company? Maybe you're an entrepreneur with a three-person company or a first-line manager in an organization that doesn't value feedback. Maybe you're not a manager at all, but an individual who sometimes serves as a technical lead and coordinates people on a project. Or you may be a professional project manager who leads and tracks cross-functional communication on many projects. In each of these cases, the higher-level bosses you report to may not have a clue that faster feedback loops will add value to their organizations. So, how do you get started with everyday feedback?

A passion for feedback

The good news is that if *you* see the benefits of everyday feedback for the team you influence, you can use it to accelerate your ability to reach your goals. Your group will shine brightly and news will spread everywhere in the organization that you're achieving great things. If you have passion and commitment for everyday feedback, you are the right person to lead and teach it into practice, even when others don't yet know how great it is.

BEVERLY ARCHER

Beverly Archer had a passion for feedback. When she moved across the country to help open up a new location for her large Silicon Valley technology company, no one else in the new location—neither recent hires nor the technical leaders who had moved with her—practiced honest communication. They stayed in their own silos and ignored people in other groups. Although Beverly began a successful feedback initiative among her team members and confronted the other managers about the need for feedback among themselves, they claimed to be "too busy for all of that," while patting her on the back as the "good corporate citizen."

When headquarters tasked the new location to double in size, things got chaotic. A huge percentage of employees complained about poor communication, feeling isolated, and the lack of development opportunities. But Beverly maintained her commitment to feedback. Her team scaled up the fastest, while maintaining positive morale. People in other groups wanted to transfer into Beverly's group because of its high morale and productivity. She persisted in giving feedback to her peer managers until they caught on and practiced everyday feedback within their small leadership team. They began to make some tough but very beneficial decisions for the new company site. They delivered a unified message about the need for developing everyone to the fullest. Headquarters applauded and morale improved. It was Beverly's insistence on feedback that made the difference.

Use metrics

Feedback becomes important when stakeholders see it moving the meter ahead on goals that matter. What's super important now in your business—sales, product invention, planning, training, reducing costs, or global expansion? Implementing competitive strategies or using smarter technologies? Feedback will be the key that opens up all of these opportunities.

Even skeptics will come to the table when they see a small manufacturing team is using faster feedback loops to dramatically reduce their cycle time. Even feedback party poopers will be impressed when they learn that feedback within the team is helping customers get happier with the company's service. Even feedback avoiders will loosen up and join in the conversation when they see that leadership development is happening in groups where managers are held accountable for everyday feedback and coaching their people.

If you want to start a feedback revolution in your company, use it to address some of the worst-performing processes in your organization—as long as they can be measured. When people are desperate for improvement and have tried different approaches, feedback can save the day. In the past, you may have avoided feedback in these difficult situations. But if you try it out and find that feedback is empowering to both employees and managers, you will be willing to open the door to the innovations that result from feedback. By leading the feedback revolution, you are helping people open up to unconventional solutions, and they are likely to see unconventionally wonderful results to follow.

Easy transition from everyday feedback with employees to peer feedback

This book has been dedicated to the urgent need for leaders to start reaping the value of faster feedback loops with the individuals they manage. I have intentionally focused on managers with direct reports because I have a mission to better the world through everyday feedback. Leaders whose jobs call for them to provide feedback will reap the benefits most immediately. But the value of feedback-based learning is huge—at all levels of the company. Teams of all types and sizes will benefit. Even team members who live remotely can connect most powerfully when the conversation is focused on shared goals, measures, and honest ideas about improvement.

A fascinating application of everyday peer feedback is in the "agile" method that has revolutionized software development teams.[42]

AGILE DEVELOPMENT AT BART'S COMPANY

The development team in Bart's company had suffered through several months of delays in getting a software solution up and running. Individuals in the group were moving in different directions and the project grew more and more complex. In response, they adopted an everyday-feedback-like practice espoused in the agile method for software development teams. The word "agile" means the ability to move quickly and cleverly with ease and grace—that is what agile principles teach. All team members attend a 10–15-minute "scrum" or meeting every morning, when everyone reports their progress and what, if anything, is blocking them. Rugby is the key metaphor used in agile as the whole team moves together, making trade-offs and solving problems as they go.[43] Feedback identifies problems, trade-offs are negotiated, and solutions are found. If a solution affects others, the team makes quick modifications. Some individuals may meet after the scrum meeting, but they do so in coordination with the whole team. As a result of this level of feedback and the information that flows freely between all team members, great progress can be made quickly.

Bart's team first began implementing the agile process as a

desperation method, as they had tried and failed a number of uncoordinated approaches. Most of the developers had preferred doing their own programming tasks and avoided the idea of daily meetings. Despite the fact that some were even vocal opponents of the agile approach, they were able to demonstrate measurable progress each week. By breaking down the project into short "sprints," they were able to give feedback every day and get everyone realigned in the most productive way possible.

Bart successfully implemented agile's feedback-intense methods by using steps similar to the everyday-feedback process with the whole group.

Peer feedback is easiest where the goal is crystal clear

In a smaller work group, where the goals and measures are easy to see, it is beneficial to shift from leader-to-employee exchanges to peer-to-peer feedback. With a common focus on a shared goal, team members have an automatic basis for conversation. They have opinions about how the goal should be achieved and ideas about how improvements can be made. If they see that something better could be implemented to achieve the shared goal, they have clear feedback to offer most members of the group. This is very much like a championship sports team. Even though there is friendly rivalry between teammates, all team members have the same goal and people are very willing to offer feedback if they think they will win or lose together. They are willing to suggest moves that will help the whole team win.

If you're part of a team where it's easy to see how everybody wins—such as in a small entrepreneurial company where everyone has a stake in the business reaching the next level—you can introduce everyday feedback easily and include peer-to-peer feedback in the mix. In situations like self-managed work teams, project teams, or where lean, Six Sigma, or other quality-improvement processes are in place, everyday feedback between team members will advance the results sought after in these flattened hierarchies.

Feedback in a small entrepreneurial company

If you are the founder of your company, you will be able to kick off feedback as soon as you hire someone. You can even use everyday feedback with contract employees; it is beneficial even if there is only one other employee in the company. You may feel a little awkward at first, introducing the idea of everyday feedback to one or two employees, but it will be powerful if you create clear ground rules and structure. In a small entrepreneurial team, everyday feedback will operate more like three equal peers talking rather than the founder acting as the boss to the others. With a small team, your vision of the company will be easily shared.

If your company has six or more employees, you may use the steps outlined earlier in the book for introducing everyday feedback. If you're a small, scrappy company, you're more likely to have people giving you feedback in response to your feedback to them. When it feels like a flatter structure with less hierarchy, people understand more easily what's going on and what's necessary for success in the whole company. Feedback loops turn at a faster rate. That is a good thing because you will be able to have great discussions about the best way to proceed.

You may be afraid that feedback will create undue conflict, but what is more often the case is that conversations about conflicting opinions lead to the best possible solutions. Only in a small percentage of cases, where an individual's personality is toxic, perhaps because of their own psychological issues, will fast feedback discussions be unproductive. In fact, everyday feedback fuels excitement. People who work for you will be very satisfied that their opinion counts and that they're invited to give feedback as well as to receive it frequently. This will be a contrast to the atmosphere in some entrepreneurial companies where feedback isn't openly given but where people are walking around trying to take hints and read the minds of the founder or another boss. In the first few months and years of a small company, it may feel as if communication is clear. But without a conscious effort to make feedback a priority, introverted technical leaders and crazed business decision makers often avoid constructive feedback and are therefore deprived of its rewards.

Building an everyday-feedback team culture

As soon as you kick off your feedback initiative, make it a team practice. After every meeting, lead some quick brainstorming about what went well in the meeting and what can be improved. Be sure to record it on a whiteboard, computer with projector, flip-chart page, or meeting software. Kick off the brainstorming with some items for improvement that you were responsible for, such as "Started late," and place your initials by them—just so the team sees you role-modeling feedback and you notice some things they could identify as feedback to you. You are priming the pump to get the feedback flowing. If people are quiet, call on them for suggestions. Note the suggestions for improvements and make a point of personally making the changes you have control over. If the feedback is for the team as a whole, such as "a few people doing all the work," ask them to clarify what they mean and use specific examples and suggestions for change. After you have personally led a few of these meetings, ask others to take turns leading regularly scheduled meetings so that they practice leadership skills and you can fully contribute.

When you are about to launch a project that involves several people in your group, conduct a "feedforward" session.[44] This has the opposite feeling of a "retrospective" or "postmortem" feedback session, where people may start talking and acting like they're disappointed. In the feedforward session, people feel empowered and excited to plan ahead for how they will create better results in the future. Although some of the conversation should naturally draw on past history to analyze exactly what needs improvement, most of the discussion will be to clarify action plans for the future. Record all of the agreed-upon plans and thread them into any project-tracking systems you are using.

Expanding feedback into all collaborative business relationships you find yourself in can be a very rewarding investment of your time and focus. Once you are using it with your direct team, there's no reason to hold back on how you work with everyone—inside and outside the organization, with people in higher or lower levels, and with cross-functional teams.

If you suggest that everyone function in an everyday-feedback way, they're likely to give it a try, see positive results on goals they care about, and quickly become feedback fans!

EVERYDAY-FEEDBACK TOOL:
Creating a special feedback counterculture

Instructions: Create the conditions for feedback success in your group even if other parts of the company aren't doing it.

1. What is your primary reason for implementing an everyday-feedback approach?

2. How can your team members explain the value of everyday feedback when asked?

3. How can you protect your team's feedback effort so that it continues to benefit individuals and the whole team?

4. When you achieve proven results from feedback, how can the team celebrate and communicate your success?

CHAPTER 15

Extra Tips for the Feedback Challenged

You may have intended to implement everyday feedback. You may have already scheduled feedback meetings or at least announced your plans to team members. But you notice that feedback is just not getting off the ground.

Chances are very high that the source of the delay is you.

Feedback is notoriously challenging. If it appears that you don't have enough time or the logistics just don't seem right, it's very likely that you are being overly cautious about giving feedback. Most logistical problems can be solved easily if you are clear that you want to do feedback and that you are ready to start—even when conditions aren't perfect.

You'll need to dig into your belief zone a little deeper to recognize barriers that still need to be moved out of the way. In figure 15.1, look for the descriptors that apply to you. They may all be located in one of the zones or they may be in several zones. After you recognize your own patterns in the chart, you'll see suggestions that address each of the zones. Read the descriptions that most apply to you. Then check out the worksheet at the end of the chapter, which can also be downloaded at www.everydayfeedback.com.

• I get a very uneasy feeling when thinking about giving corrective feedback to people on my team. • I have some people who may be volatile, so I'm concerned about the effects of feedback on them. • Regular written communication should be able to cover feedback issues, and I am extremely uncomfortable with frequent verbal conversations for the purpose of feedback. • I'm very concerned about appearing inconsistent with the way I've handled feedback in the past. • In general, I am uncomfortable communicating to people who may act emotional about their feedback. **Analyzer**	• I'm ready to fire, demote, or change the duties of some of my people, and I don't want the feedback to give them a false sense of encouragement. • My employees are choosing not to perform in areas they're accountable for, and I refuse to let that make us fail to achieve our goals. • I'm uncomfortable having personal conversations with the people on my team. • Feedback is an extreme waste of time. I tell everyone what's expected in meetings and in goal-setting conversations at the beginning of the year. I don't feel that I should spend more time giving feedback. • Feedback is like parenting. I feel like my people are responsible adults who should not need coddling. **Changer**
Empathizer 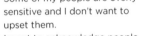 • Some of my people are overly sensitive and I don't want to upset them. • I want to acknowledge people who are trying hard, even if they don't quite meet their goals. • Feedback could get in the way of my close relationships with my team members. • I've never been comfortable giving feedback to friends, family members , or coworkers. • I am concerned that people will become demotivated if I give corrective feedback.	**Motivator** 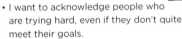 • Things are changing fast in the company right now, and I don't want to demoralize people with negative feedback. • I think the team dynamic is strong and the team members can give each other feedback better than I can. • I'm concerned about appearing unfair because I would give some people more corrective feedback and others more praise. • We have great morale on our team right now and feedback conversations would decrease morale. • I have occasion to work more closely with some more than others on my team, so it's hard to give feedback consistently to everyone.

Figure 15.1. Zone-based challenges

Suggestions for the feedback-challenged Analyzer

If most of your challenges fall in the Analyzer category, you may be temperamentally reluctant to step into any feedback situations.

Because you are more comfortable with fact-based conversations, you may be concerned that any feedback comment you make will be interpreted as subjective and personal. You are also very sensitive to out-of-control reactions that, in your view, are quite possible within a feedback conversation. You may perceive that spontaneous or unstructured face-to-face feedback conversations are more likely than written reviews to cause misinterpretation and emotional reactions.

The good news for you is that if you can get feedback off the ground, you will actually decrease the risk of overly emotional responses from people. If you invite frequent, short feedback discussions with your team members and ask for their opinions, you will find that it leads them to a better understanding of the facts and to the desire to draw more logical conclusions. Feedback, as scary as it sounds, can actually provide you with a better understanding of facts and help you make better decisions than when you operate in isolation from such conversations.

1. Be deliberate in starting your feedback conversations with people who are easy to talk to and whose emotional reactions you are not worried about.

2. Try, as a test case, giving feedback just to one person before even thinking about announcing it to other people. This is usually not good advice, as you don't want anyone to feel singled out, but there is probably somebody in your group—a great performer, for instance—who craves feedback and would naturally benefit from it.

3. When you do announce your feedback plans in a meeting for your whole team, you can prevent the likelihood of emotional reactions by giving them a heads up for what you will discuss. Kick it off by saying there have been several themes that have come up for everybody: "We tend to be good in some areas, but there are others where we need specific improvements on

project deadlines, communicating project status, and keeping everyone apprised of problems." So, essentially you are preventing surprises in your subsequent meetings with everyone and thereby preventing anyone from being caught off guard by defensive responses from employees.

4. Prepare in advance. You will be far more comfortable if you write a COIN script for each conversation you set up in the initial feedback round and for each informal feedback conversation you have for the next four to six conversations thereafter. (Use the forms from the end of chapter 9, downloadable from www.everydayfeedback.com.)

Suggestions for the feedback-challenged Charger

If you find your feedback challenges to be in the Charger category, you are impatient with feedback conversations. Although you are already likely to be giving corrective feedback—and plenty of it— you may be impatient with the Connection, Impact, and Next Steps parts of the COIN feedback model. You may not be giving much—or any—positive feedback, and if you are giving some attaboys, you are probably skipping over all four parts of COIN on the positive feedback. The fact is, most managers outside this zone are happy to talk to employees about positive things, and it may actually make you impatient with them as you believe they are misusing a lot of their time.

We don't want to force you into doing something you don't believe in. You really need to take a time-out from your feedback plan and conduct an experiment. Test it out on one or two people you've been frustrated with in the past. See if using the full COIN model in your conversations with these employees will lead to something you do care about—results.

Once you are convinced that everyday feedback is a good thing, you may still be concerned about time management. Because you are impatient to complete as many tasks as possible in as short a time frame as possible, one of your challenges will be finding time to talk to everyone. A key to this is realizing that a feedback conversation, when it hits on the key themes that are important to the person and to the business, will be quite fast and you will not need to spend as much time on it as you think.

1. Slow down your feedback plans for the whole team if you aren't convinced it's worth your time. Try it out on a person who doesn't seem to be getting the message, someone you've given corrective feedback to and whose performance is below par. Test out the full COIN model, but write out a COIN script first.

2. For the Connect step in COIN, do not even attempt "happy talk" that is unnatural to you. Such play-acting will seem fake from you and it won't work. Instead, find a business topic that you know they are interested in to use as your icebreaker. Get them engaged in something of real interest to both of you as a way to connect more naturally. Show authentic interest in something of their world.

3. For the Impact step in COIN, be patient about the fact that the other person really does not understand the impact of their actions. You will need to explain the business goals that they are impacting. How does their behavior toward customers affect business measures like repeat business? How does their failure to communicate expected delays affect the project and its costs? How does their lack of feedback to their team members affect turnover costs and quality? Since you inhabit the Charger zone, you know what results you are looking for, but

you will need to explain them in a way they can understand and commit to.

4. For the Next Step in COIN, ask for their ideas on how to solve the problem. Avoid dictating your solution, and praise the ideas that are workable in their proposed solutions.

5. After observing the changes (or lack of changes) in this person's performance, decide for yourself whether the feedback discussion is worth spreading to your whole team. If it is, make sure you communicate your intentions to the whole team.

Suggestions for the feedback-challenged Empathizer

As an Empathizer, it may be painful for you to be asked to do what you consider to be inflicting pain on people. Your whole challenge is to explore how constructive feedback and helpful coaching from you are a gift you are giving your employees.

Your focus will be to separate out your memories or beliefs about feedback being a painful and negative process. Your turnaround on this will occur when you can see feedback as helpful and appreciated.

1. Review chapter 8 ("Step 2: "Look for the 'Highest Good'"), as it tees up your feedback campaign with positive images of your team succeeding. Spend extra time applying this step or do it repeatedly, at least once a week for three weeks, before resuming your feedback plan.

2. Interview three people in your group about their attitudes about feedback. Select an "eager beaver" great performer, a steady performer who wants to improve, and a slower performer. Ask each of them about their feedback preference— whether they want people to be honest with them when they

have feedback, or whether they prefer to wait once a year for a written performance review. You will notice that at least two out of the three will welcome an everyday-feedback approach.

3. Once you are determined to move ahead on your everyday-feedback plan, write out COIN scripts using the worksheet you can download from www.everydayfeedback.com. Since you are already accomplished in the Connection step, figure out how to move through it a little more quickly and spend the bulk of your time on the other three steps.

4. Make sure you are clear on your specific Observations and business Impact statements. You may have to think about these a little more and plan how you will explain them before going into your meetings.

5. After you've done a first round of everyday feedback, ask people how they are working and note how appreciative many of your direct reports will be.

Suggestions for the feedback-challenged Motivator

As a Motivator, you may already think your feedback approach is working and you may not see how your lack of specifics and inconsistency are underserving your people. But you are dissatisfied with not yet reaching your exciting goals for the future. You are already a great communicator and you may be convinced that diving into the specifics with every single member of your team is worth the effort.

Your personal challenge will be to convince yourself that everyday feedback is worth spending your time and energy on. Once you are convinced, you will need to find a way to stay focused and structured enough to make it happen. The rest is easy. Once you are doing it regularly, you will incorporate it enthusiastically into your plans and become a cheerleader for the value of feedback!

1. Test out the everyday-feedback approach with the one or two people who can most help you jump forward on the goals you are so excited about. What is your most important goal that you hope to reach in less than a year? Who are the one or two people who are most critical to helping the team achieve this goal? Go through the COIN process with each of them, making sure to fulfill the O, I, and N steps in a thorough and structured way. You are already good at the Connect and part of the Next Steps actions in the model.

2. Before meeting with these one or two people, think, plan, and draft scripts for each. Make sure your Observations are precise. On what occasions did the behaviors occur? What exactly did they do or fail to do?

3. Explain the Impact clearly. How does their behavior (or lack of behavior) affect the goal you are trying to achieve? If they don't understand the goal, explain it in more detail.

4. Make sure that Next Steps are clear and agreed upon. Write them down while you are still in the conversation with your employee. Agree that either you or the employee will summarize and email the Next Steps to the other person.

5. Make a commitment to the employee that you will follow up with the Next Steps about a week later so that both of you take these plans seriously.

6. Within a month, notice if your goal is being affected positively. It is likely to be moving forward, and if so, make plans to spread the everyday feedback to the whole team.

7. Feel free to be a feedback cheerleader throughout your company!

EVERYDAY-FEEDBACK TOOL:
Your feedback challenge zones

Instructions:

1. The four zones are listed below. For each category, rate each challenge (0–5) based on how applicable it is to you—the higher the number, the more applicable.
2. Enter the total for each category. Identify the category with the highest and second highest score. In some cases you will have a tie for either highest or second highest total.
3. Reread all of the sections in this chapter that apply to you.

 **Analyzer**

	I get a very uneasy feeling when thinking about giving corrective feedback to people on my team.
	I have some people who may be volatile, so I'm concerned about the effects of feedback on them.
	Regular written communication should be able to cover feedback issues, and I am extremely uncomfortable with frequent verbal conversations for the purpose of feedback.
	I'm very concerned about appearing inconsistent with the way I've handled feedback in the past.
	In general, I am uncomfortable communicating to people who may act emotional about their feedback.
Total:	

 **Charger**

	I'm ready to fire, demote, or change the duties of some of my people, and I don't want the feedback to give them a false sense of encouragement.
	My employees are choosing not to perform in areas they're accountable for, and I refuse to let that make us fail to achieve our goals.
	I'm uncomfortable having personal conversations with the people on my team.
	Feedback is an extreme waste of time. I tell everyone what's expected at the beginning of the year. I don't feel that I should spend more time giving feedback.
	Feedback is like parenting. I feel like my people are responsible adults who should not need coddling.
Total:	

 Empathizer

	Some of my people are overly sensitive, and I don't want to upset them.
	I want to acknowledge people who are trying hard, even if they don't quite meet their goals.
	Feedback could get in the way of my close relationships with my team members.
	I've never been comfortable giving feedback to friends, family members, or coworkers.
	I am concerned that people will become demotivated if I give corrective feedback.
Total:	

 **Motivator**

	Things are changing fast in the company right now, and I don't want to demoralize people with negative feedback.
	I think the team dynamic is strong and team members can give each other feedback better than I can.
	I'm concerned about appearing unfair because I would give some people more corrective feedback and others more praise.
	We have great morale on our team right now and feedback conversations would decrease morale.
	I have occasion to work more closely with some more than others on my team, so it's hard to give feedback consistently to everyone.
Total:	

Leaping Ahead from Your Feedback Loops

In the first chapter, I relayed my conversation with Gerald, a leader who was poised to fire someone his company had spent a lot of time and money hiring. I am happy to report that Gerald decided to hold off on the firing and embark on a feedback journey with the VP, Tony. Through their many everyday-feedback conversations that followed, both Gerald and Tony reached a much clearer understanding of how each of them could be most successful in their roles. Gerald was able to explain the full impact—both the positive and negative—of Tony's key actions, and at Gerald's invitation, Tony supplied Gerald with feedback to improve his impact as a CEO. Both enjoyed their thought-provoking conversations, grew immensely in their roles, and finished out the year successfully, leading their company to high growth in a changing market.

I don't want to leave the impression that separating someone from your company is always bad. In some situations, it is the very best course of action and may be the fastest route to company improvement and higher morale. But giving feedback to everyone who works for you—at all levels of their membership on your team—will always help. By following an everyday-feedback approach with everyone, you can motivate high performers, improve performance, and in the rare situations where termination is needed, get it done faster and more smoothly. Poor performers may loop themselves right out of your organization when they know what is expected and realize they cannot or will not meet those standards. You just can't go wrong by practicing everyday feedback and building an environment in which feedback is a high-priority value.

Feedback about feedback

As Gerald reflected on how much he had learned from giving and receiving feedback, he realized he had been advancing from his own feedback loops. He had begun with a piece of new *information*, that there was another option he could try to help him get the results he wanted. He made *adjustments* in his behavior, initiating direct conversations with Carla about how she could work better and smarter in this particular organization. He saw positive *results*—"Aha, this is working!"—which became the new information to feed his motivation toward even more everyday feedback with Carla and others on his team.

Your own feedback loop of learning

If you've followed the everyday-feedback process thus far, you've already cycled through many feedback loops of learning. By applying the six steps for your different people—for new hires, old hands, superstars, strugglers, hardworking contributors, and yourself— you're now in a position to make an association between the information, adjustments, and results in your own feedback loop.

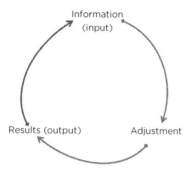

Figure 16.1. The feedback loop

Take a look at your own feedback loops and trace what you have learned about the process of everyday feedback with your team members. What are your biggest surprises? What are you most excited about, and what do you want to practice and get better at?

I have asked these questions to many leaders. After trying out everyday feedback, leaders frequently discover that *honest feedback— done in a helpful way—dramatically speeds up learning between people.*

Once people get a clearer picture of what will work better, they are actually happy to change what they are doing right away! Employees are often working a certain way because they simply don't know how to perform differently. A very high percentage of employees want to be successful at their jobs, and when they can see a route to being more successful, they behave differently.

Actions based on feedback can be a huge driver of success for the company

Even small changes in the way my team members treat customers or colleagues, even small increases in the amount of time my first line managers spend meeting with their teams, and even the slow but genuine progress I make in following my employees' feedback all make a visible impact. This visible impact motivates me to try more, give better feedback, and build momentum toward greater and greater impact.

My brain calmed down when I saw that feedback was the opposite of scary—I actually enjoyed helping people

Although I was very uncomfortable getting started on my everyday-feedback routine, I quickly changed my whole attitude about it. Some of my employees actually told me they had been hoping for frequent feedback for a long time and they were so grateful that I had shown the courage to initiate it. As I got into it more and more, I saw that people had been hungry for the honesty that I had been avoiding so much.

Feedback isn't time consuming; it actually saves time

Once my team members and I put our cards on the table, exchanged helpful feedback, and established trust, we spent much less time tiptoeing around tough issues and figuring out how to avoid people's defensive reactions. The route to improvement became a direct one, with no time-consuming detours. Sometimes the fastest route to success has included sharing our differences of opinion about the best path to business success; those conversations have been a good expenditure of our time. We have built an environment that welcomes everyday feedback, and there has only been an increase in our efficiency.

I have become a better leader as a result of my everyday-feedback conversations

Since the job of a leader is to get things done through other people, I must stay focused on what I can do to expedite and assist others in their work. This is my task, even though our environment is changing so fast that I feel compelled to stop and do some of the work myself. I have to remember that everyday feedback keeps me involved in coaching conversations with my team members, and that is the most effective thing I do as a leader to have a great impact.

As you review your own feedback loops on what everyday feedback has accomplished for you, I believe you will report positive results for yourself personally—by lightening the stress you may have expected, speaking your own truth to others, feeling the gratification of developing others to do more than they thought possible, and experiencing exciting business wins.

Frequently Asked Questions

As you implement and pursue everyday feedback, you may run into some interesting challenges. Here are some frequently asked questions:

Giving feedback to emotional, confrontational, or toxic employees

Q: I have an employee who can be emotional and angry sometimes. What if I don't think the person can handle feedback?

A: A small percentage of your team members may react defensively when you mention any feedback that implies the need to improve. This can be prevented by demonstrating that you "see" them and acknowledge the good things that they are doing. When they feel fully recognized and realize that you're telling them the truth about the good things, they may be more willing to hear about areas needing improvement.

You may be frustrated with these people because their poor performance has gone on a long time. But you're both starting a new journey together. It's important to take one step at a time, break the feedback down into workable improvement goals, and remain calm. Since this is the first time you are fully addressing the problems, it's as if the behavior has occurred for the first time as well.

For these folks, even more than for others, you should avoid global statements like "You aren't service oriented when you're dealing with customers." That feels like a personal attack and they're bound to be defensive. Find some specific examples of the behavior in question and be extra careful to pick out a Goldilocks-sized chunk that's just right for them to work on.

Focus on the behavior you want them to improve in the future. Direct them toward the goal that they will be working on over the next few weeks, and request that they spend more time developing a good relationship with customers and asking questions, rather than jumping in with comments that would irritate customers.

Make sure that you walk in with a calm state of mind and remain calm no matter how they react. Bringing it back to the goals of the team and how you would like them to develop reframes the conversation to the big picture and gets you out of the weeds of arguing with them over technicalities. If they act defensively, it's essential that you not act defensively. If they appear angry, ask a probing question: "What's the worst part of this conversation for you?" or "How can you increase customer satisfaction?" The more defensive they are, the more questions you should ask, but it's also important that you stay centered in your own concern, as a leader, for the performance of the whole team.

Q: I have an employee who is good in one technical area but has a toxic personality—he can't get along with coworkers, and he receives customer complaints if allowed to take customer service calls. How can I frame feedback for this person, as he wants to know how to get ahead in the company?

A: What's so great about the everyday-feedback process is that you can focus on one skill area at a time and gradually help him build the needed capability. Take the time to explore what he is puzzled about and the meaning behind his words. Of course you're going to have both positive and corrective feedback about the skill areas needed for the role. Share feedback that is honest and focused on examples of current behavior. If customers are complaining about how they were handled rudely, you can share, "I got a call from a customer and they mentioned feeling put down in the way you answered their question. Let's explore that situation." You might suggest some sample phrases for how to handle it differently. You could even do a little role-playing over several feedback sessions to help him get the feel of a more positive way of handling customer complaints (or whatever the issue at hand).

This begins a discovery process between you and the employee—for the purpose of his growing, changing, and fully understanding where he still has barriers.

A giver of everyday feedback is never patronizing; such a manager avoids thinking, *I know what's best for you, and I'm going to steer you to jobs you can handle and avoid things I think you can't handle.* Instead we are being open and honest, answering concerns, and giving advice on their own goals. If the person with the toxic personality wants to move into a focused customer service role where you don't think he would be effective, you must make sure that you have given him feedback in those areas of customer effectiveness that would let him know honestly what's going well, what's still not working, and where he still needs to improve.

This is a fascinating topic because, in many organizations, managers and management in general decide who does not have potential for a particular job, yet they never discuss these issues openly with the people who want to get ahead. If the employees don't know why they are repeatedly passed over for a promotion, they don't have the opportunity to improve their approach.

Q: I have an employee who used some of our feedback time to tattle on other people on the team and tell me how much more conscientious she is than they are.

A: Follow COIN and redirect the employee to focus on her role. Tell her what she is doing effectively and what she can improve. Give feedback about open communication with the entire group and your desire to reduce gossip and indirect communication about other people. So, you might say, "I'd like to suggest that you focus your conversations on your own experiences and job interests, as well as offering feedback to me about how I can help you do a better job. If you have advice for the team, I welcome you to give the feedback in our team meetings or with the individual team members involved rather than talking with me about them."

Q: I noticed that after I asked people to give feedback, one employee used it as an opportunity to be rude and insulting toward me and other team members.

A: In your individual feedback with this person, mention your definition of feedback and how it should be helpful to the people involved, whether it is positive reinforcement or improvement feedback. Show this person the COIN model, and remind them that they should use feedback to provide helpful information they can use to change what they are doing. Give them examples of the rude comments you heard in the meeting and the negative effects that it had on you, other team members, and them personally. Follow the COIN process yourself in giving this feedback.

Feedback to low performers / nonperformers

Q: How do I deal with a very low performer whose work I've never really addressed in performance reviews?

A: This is a tricky question because one aspect of the improvement that you want to make is in your own behavior; just the giving of feedback now is a breakthrough moment. You can't correct years of poor performance in one feedback session. Think of an important task that they are responsible for and think of some milestones they should reach in the next few weeks. Focus on areas that you can point to in the recent past where there were problems, and then describe how they can improve in the future. That way, they don't feel attacked and you have a "chunk of behavior" that can be worked on. Remind yourself that the feedback process is ongoing and that as they learn and achieve milestones in one area, they will be more eager and trusting of you as they tackle additional areas of improvement.

Q: I have a team member who completes their tasks quite well, but does not help other team members with their projects. This is a problem because we are stretched thin and need everyone to pitch in and collaborate.

A: What's so great about everyday feedback is that you can explain some of the criteria or competencies necessary for your team's success as part of what you are expecting from an individual. In this case you need everyone to pitch in and collaborate. Give this person feedback about what you have observed in regard to their lack of collaboration and its impact on the whole team. You might say, "Collaboration is a major competency for everyone in our group. You finished your project for the week, but didn't pitch in to help with our big, ongoing project that the others were focused on. Our team came in a day late and we had to apologize to the customer. I request that you be flexible on our future projects and offer to help on unfinished tasks."

Q: One of my direct reports doesn't like the tasks involved in his role. He would prefer to take on tasks that involve more communication with other people in the company and be less focused on technical accuracy of his assigned job tasks. He barely meets expectations in his current position and requires a lot of learning and improvement in the current job.

A: Explore with him what his career aspirations are, discuss what those other roles require, and give him feedback on his current performance. Share with him the possibilities for any kind of promotion or transfer, but make sure to emphasize the true requirements. Very often jobs that appear to be exciting from the outside involve more of a technical focus than one thinks. In most situations, he would need to master the ability to focus, learn, and be most effective in his current role before he can be qualified for the next role. Be sure to remind him that there is always the possibility that he would do well with another role and explain exactly what such a move would entail. Take it slow and don't be defensive. Try to frame issues with his current role in the context of team and company goals rather than your personal judgment about his unrealistic thinking.

Feedback to remote or less accessible employees

Q: What about giving feedback to remote employees whom I don't see in person very often?

A: Since you don't see these folks as often and don't have the close working conditions, eye contact, or informal conversations, it's even more important that you begin phone contact with them on a more frequent basis in order to build more rapport. When you give feedback, it may actually take you a little longer than with others because there is a lack of face-to-face communication. The trust that you build will pay off, but you may notice that it requires a little more attention than when you talk to people in the hallway on a day-to-day basis. If you do have personal contact in the same city—even if it's infrequent—be sure to plan dinner, lunch, or extended meetings so you can get to know them better, and use those opportunities for providing some everyday feedback. Allocate time to solicit their feedback to you, and let them know that you value their suggestions.

The guidelines for everyday feedback are really the same for out-of-town people as for face-to-face connections, so don't let these folks slip away and feel "out of sight, out of mind." Send them short, frequent notes and plenty of positive messages. Call to get more input than usual from them. You will find that they will be very happy to have the increased communication initiated by you.

You may wonder how you can track what they are doing. This can be part of the feedback process, in which you explore with them how they are handling their assignments, and you can offer feedback on the approaches they describe. For instance, if they are contracting with suppliers in a foreign city, ask them how that relationship is going, how they set up the arrangements with them, and how they're managing the contractors. You may want to give some feedback, both positive and improvement feedback, on the examples they give you and how they are performing in general.

This is like a behavioral event interview that you might conduct with a job candidate. You're asking them to tell stories about what they have actually done. But, in the case of remote employees, you are using their descriptive stories as your observations of their behavior. Of course, you'll want to have other performance parameters: metrics and input from customers, colleagues, and other managers. This can work quite well and the feedback can be the basis for better business conversations with people in remote locations. They will feel closer and not so isolated from the main office or from wherever you are.

Managing time for giving feedback

Q: If a team member comes into my office and asks for feedback often, how do I keep from spending too much time with her?

A: While there are some eager beavers (often they're the younger ones on the team) who want constant feedback, your new approach allows you to give quick and frequent feedback. It's OK to let them know that you don't have a lot of time available, but that you do enjoy frequent interactions with them. It's also fine to provide them a bit more feedback than other people are getting, as long as it fits into your schedule. After they realize you are being authentic and helpful, they will trust you and relax a bit.

Giving feedback when other leaders don't do it

Q: My peers don't give their people much feedback. Won't I be seen as the harshest boss if I do feedback so frequently?

A: It is true that your employees will fan out into the organization and let other people and other groups know that they are receiving feedback frequently. There may be some raised eyebrows from their peers, who might make comments like "I'm glad I'm not in that group." These peers will share with their managers what is going on in your group, but it's really not a worry. Precisely because people become more engaged when they are having more frequent dialogues with you, they are probably not going to present these conversations in a negative light. There may be a few exceptions to this, but others will also know that the naysayers aren't representative of everyone in their group. Your peers will likely admire you and want to know how you achieved everyday feedback.

Working on feedback skills

Q: How can I get better at my feedback role?

A: Your process of giving feedback is also one big feedback loop. You are constantly adjusting the way you give feedback so that you can achieve better results and have more engaged employees. Notice what's working and what's not working so well, make notes as you go through the first round of feedback discussions, and observe what changes people make as a result of the feedback. Notice what they appreciate when they come in to talk to you again or when you talk to them the second time. Notice how proud or puzzled they are when they are able to make the changes you proposed. Use the COIN tool to write yourself another round of scripts that improve on the ones that you've used the last time. Make sure that you bite off the right-sized chunk of behavior for your team member and that the two of you are committed to solutions that will improve their performance. Ask them how the feedback is going for them and how you can improve the way you give feedback; be sure to record everything they say so that you can adjust your own feedback process.

*Q: What are the pros and cons of setting up a 360°
feedback process to get input about my leadership?*
A: 360° feedback is always a great opportunity when it's available. Your company may have a leadership-development program that includes 360° feedback. 360° helps you identify a few key areas to focus on so that you can receive the greatest benefit from coaching.

All of this is great, but nothing beats ongoing dialogue with the people who give you face-to-face feedback where they can provide real-time examples and clarify the details you need. Sometimes 360° feedback is considered a "be all, end all" single solution for feedback to leaders. But it is only a starting point. The fact that these surveys are anonymous is often the reason given for why the feedback is so great. What I've seen in many years of consulting is that honest feedback given face to face trumps 360° feedback because of the give and take that's possible from this kind of conversation. The feedback that comes from "behind the mask" is limited because there's never enough explanation or examples. The leader may be perplexed about whom and in what situation the feedback is referring to and it seems isolated from specific work goals. It does not foster trust, which is cultivated during everyday feedback. In face-to-face conversations you are investing in an ongoing pursuit of more trust and helpful feedback between the two of you in the future.

Giving feedback to high achievers

Q: I have a couple of eager beavers in my group who constantly push me for a promotion. How can I use everyday feedback to help them be a little more patient?

A: First of all, explore with them what roles they want, and have an honest discussion about the kinds of skills and knowledge needed for promotion to those roles. Employees are often surprised to learn of the competencies that are required for a higher-level role. These higher capabilities may not be required for their current role and you may not yet have observed them demonstrating these skills. Sometimes it's just enough for them to realize, "Whoa, I really need to learn more about that," and they become more realistic about what it takes to get ahead.

They are also using this opportunity to express the desire for a promotion and giving you feedback that they want you to immediately promote them. You should be honest. Be clear about the company's goals, what jobs are available, and management's thinking about how they are planning to fill those jobs, if those positions happen to be open. If there are particular job openings outside your area that they are interested in, you can help them explore the specific job requirements. You can offer feedback for them focusing on the required skills that they have or don't have and help them grow. Of course, if they are qualified for a promotion and you think that they would be good in the new role, you should recommend them for the promotion.

Overall, be authentic, be honest, and share as much information as you can about what it takes to achieve the promotion. The rapport that you are building with them in the everyday-feedback relationship is mentoring them in career development. If they continue to want a promotion and are almost demanding that a promotion occur right away, spend some time going over what people—inside and outside the company—have done to reach that level. When they realize, for instance, that the advanced degree they don't have is required for a position they want, they will likely calm down, become more patient, and solicit your help in getting the education needed.

Q: Won't my best people become demotivated if I keep mentioning areas they could improve upon?

A: It's usually the contrary. People who are high performers are often confident about their work and will respond positively to your suggestions. People who are excellent at what they do enjoy challenges and are usually eager to "take it up a notch." They're usually willing to test out new ways of doing things and are not emotionally crestfallen when someone gives them improvement feedback. Based on research on employee engagement, we know that the best people will feel happier in an environment where they are asked to think and grow and where they are engaged in a dialogue with their manager. If they're truly great employees, they won't be defensive about the changes that you're suggesting. If they don't feel the changes that you're suggesting are appropriate, they will be able to give you convincing reasons why those changes may not be the best solutions. Your conversations with high performers are likely to be very fulfilling and educational for both of you.

Notes

Chapter 1

[1] "Welcome to Gamification WiKi," www.gamification.org.

[2] Kevin Kelly, *Out of Control: The New Biology of Machines, Social Systems & the Economic World* (New York: Basic Books, 1995).

[3] Debra Donston-Miller, "7 Examples: Put Gamification to Work," *Information Week*, May 2012.

[4] Anna Carroll, "Everyday Feedback Workshop," October 2013.

[5] Gallup, *Survey on Employee Engagement*, 2011.

[6] Leadership IQ Study, "Employees Want Feedback, Even if It's Negative, Study Finds," *World at Work*, October 9, 2009.

Chapter 2

[7] Jeanne C. Meister and Karie Willyerd, "Mentoring Millennials," *Harvard Business Review*, May 2010.

[8] Jay Gilbert, "The Millennials: A New Generation of Employees, A New Set of Engagement Policies," *Ivey Business Journal* (September/October 2011).

[9] Ibid.

[10] Janet Choi, "How Radical Transparency Kills Stress," *Fast Company*, July 2013.

[11] Clive Thompson, "The See-Through CEO," *Wired*, March 2007.

[12] Cornerstone OnDemand, "Harris 2012 US Employee Report."

[13] Ton Agan, "Embracing the Millennials' Mind-Set at Work," *New York Times*, November 9, 2013.

[14] Joanne Sujansky and Jan Ferri-Reed, *Keeping the Millennials: Why Companies Are Losing Billions in Turnover to This Generation—and What to Do About It* (Hoboken: Wiley, 2009).

[15] Glenn Llopis, "5 Powerful Things Happen When a Leader Is Transparent," *Forbes*, September 10, 2012.

Chapter 3

[16] David Rock, "Managing with the Brain in Mind," *strategy + business*, August 29, 2009.

Chapter 4

[17] The Myers Briggs Foundation, http://www.myersbriggs.org/my-mbti-personality-type/mbti-basics/isabel-briggs-myers.asp; Tracom Group, http://www.tracomcorp.com/training-products/model/social-style-model.html; Insights Learning and Development Limited, www.insights.com/564/insights-discovery.html.

Chapter 5

[18] Charles Jacobs, *Management Rewired: Why Feedback Doesn't Work and Other Surprising Lessons from the Latest Brain Science*, reprint edition (New York: Portfolio, 2009).

[19] Ibid.

[20] David Rock, "Managing with the Brain in Mind."

[21] Daniel Goleman, *The Brain and Emotional Intelligence: New Insights*, Kindle edition (Florence, MA: More Than Sound, 2011).

[22] George Altman, "The Mirror in Us: Mirror Neurons & Workplace Relationships," *The Intentional Workplace*, January 19, 2012; Daniel Goleman, *Social Intelligence: The New Science of Human Relationships* (New York: Bantam, 2007).

[23] Goleman, *The Brain and Emotional Intelligence.*

[24] David Rock and Jeffrey Schwartz, "The Neuroscience of Leadership," *strategy + business*, May 30, 2006; Monty McKeever, "The Brain and Emotional Intelligence: An Interview with Daniel Goleman," *Tricycle*, May 18, 2011, http://www.tricycle.com/blog/brain-and-emotional-intelligence-interview-daniel-goleman.

[25] David Rock, "The Neuroscience of Mindfulness," *Psychology Today*, October 2009.

[26] Rock and Schwartz, "The Neuroscience of Leadership."

Chapter 6

[27] Leigh Branham, "The Seven Hidden Reasons Employees Leave," ASAE, *Executive Update Magazine*, February 2005.

[28] Gallup, *Survey on Employee Engagement*, 2011.

[29] Cornerstone OnDemand, *Harris 2012 US Employee Report.*

[30] Cornerstone OnDemand, *Harris 2012 US Employee Report.*

[31] Rachel Emma Silverman, "Yearly Reviews? Try Weekly: Accustomed to Updates, New Generation of Workers Craves Regular Feedback," *Wall Street Journal*, September 6, 2011.

[32] Meister and Willyerd, "Mentoring Millennials."

[33] Josh Bersin, "Time to Scrap Performance Appraisals?" *Forbes*, May 2013.

[34] Samuel A. Culbert, "Get Rid of the Performance Review!" *Wall Street Journal*, October 2008.

[35] Daniel Pink, *Drive: The Surprising Truth About What Motivates Us* (New York: Riverhead Books, 2011).

Chapter 8
[36] Daniel Pink, *Drive*.

Chapter 10
[37] David Rock, "Managing with the Brain in Mind."
[38] Daniel Debow, "When You're the Boss, Who Gives You Reviews?" *Fortune*/CNN, December 22, 2010.
[39] Amy Gallo, "How to Get Feedback When You're the Boss," *Harvard Business Review*, HBR Blog Network, May 2012.

Chapter 13
[40] Marshall Goldsmith, "6 Questions for Better Coaching," *Huffington Post*, August 2009.
[41] James O'Toole and Warren Bennis, "A Culture of Candor," *Harvard Business Review*, June 2009.

Chapter 14
[42] Andrew Fuqua, "What Do Scrum Teams Do During the Release Sprint?" *Leading Agile*, November 2013.
[43] Salah Elleithy, "Agile Transformation: The 3 Key Ingredients," *Project Times*, May 2013.
[44] Marshall Goldsmith, *Feedforward* (Highland Park, IL: Writers of the Round Table Press, 2012).

Index

About the Author

Anna Carroll, MSSW, is an organization development consultant, facilitator, coach, and speaker. Through her practice, Interaction Design, Inc., she has designed and led training and group planning experiences and has created learning tools and assessments to speed up group success with clients such as Applied Materials, Austin Regional Clinic, eBay, GE, Horseshoe Bay Resort, Houghton Mifflin Harcourt, Starwood Hotels, University of Texas, and Zimmer.

Most recently Carroll has focused on the power of feedback loops and how leaders and team members can overcome their barriers to exchanging valuable feedback in the workplace. Her website is www.EverydayFeedback.com. She lives in Austin, Texas, with her husband Michael Wilkes.

Made in the
USA
Middletown, DE